CONTENTS

KU-595-555

About the author

Frances Butler is a visiting research fellow at ippr working on human rights and equalities issues. She is also a member of the task force advising government on arrangements to establish the commission for equality and human rights and a specialist adviser to the Parliamentary Joint Committee on Human Rights. She is the editor of *Human Rights Protection: Methods and Effectiveness* (British Institute of Human Rights/Kluwer 2001), vice president of the British Institute of Human Rights and a member of the executive board of Liberty.

Acknowledgements

The author would like to thank the following people for their contributions to the project and thoughtful comments on the draft report: Tabby Collingbourne; Sarah Cooke (British Institute of Human Rights); Gillian Fawcett (Audit Commission); Teresa Gorczynska; Tessa Harding (Help the Aged); Francesca Klug (LSE Centre for Human Rights); Sue Regan (Shelter); Campbell Robb (NCVO); Laura Roling (Comic Relief); Sandy Ruxton (Oxfam); Carol Sexty and Guy Cave (Save the Children UK); Sarah Spencer (Centre on Migration, Policy and Society); Jenny Watson (human rights consultant); and Rob Williamson (Northern Rock Foundation).

This project was made possible by the generosity of Comic Relief and thanks also go to Northern Rock Foundation who kindly provided facilities for the seminar in Newcastle.

Colleagues at ippr always provide sound advice and thanks are due to: Kate Stanley, Howard Reed, Will Paxton and John Adams. John Schwartz, Kate Lewandowska, Abigail Rowe and Katya Collaut also provided much-needed support.

Grateful thanks are especially due to the many individuals who gave so freely of their time to participate in this project whether by attending the seminars, responding to the questionnaire or in telephone conversations with the author. Their considerable expertise and wealth of experience have proved invaluable in producing this report and their contributions are much appreciated.

HUMAN RIGHTS: WHO NEEDS THEM?

USING HUMAN RIGHTS IN THE VOLUNTARY SECTOR

FRANCES BUTLER

The ippr

The **Institute for Public Policy Research** (ippr) is the UK's leading progressive think tank and was established in 1988. Its role is to bridge the political divide between the social democratic and liberal traditions, the intellectual divide between academia and the policy making establishment and the cultural divide between government and civil society. It is first and foremost a research institute, aiming to provide innovative and credible policy solutions. Its work, the questions its research poses and the methods it uses are driven by the belief that the journey to a good society is one that places social justice, democratic participation and economic and environmental sustainability at its core.

For further information you can contact ippr's external affairs department on info@ippr.org, you can view our website at www.ippr.org and you can buy our books from Central Books on 0845 458 9910 or email ippr@centralbooks.com.

Our trustees

Executive summary

Britain enjoys a mature democracy, a healthy economy and a vibrant civil society. Despite those advantages, poverty and social exclusion endure, and are an abiding concern for social progressives. Political will and the application of resources and commitment are required if the goal of equality and social justice is to be achieved. There are several mechanisms that exist for that purpose such as provision under the welfare state, initiatives to relieve poverty and laws targeting discrimination against particular groups. But socio-economic deprivation is also typically accompanied by inadequate public services, poor treatment and discrimination. As a result, disadvantaged people can experience lack of respect, disregard for their dignity and powerlessness. What can human rights contribute to remedying these deficiencies?

The Human Rights Act provides a legal basis for protecting certain rights that civilised countries take for granted. These include the right to life, liberty, fair hearing, private and family life, freedom of conscience, religion, expression and association and freedom from degrading treatment and discrimination. These rights are founded on the universal principles of equality, dignity and respect and the desire for social progress. They, like the mechanisms already referred to, have a part to play in achieving greater social justice. Human rights principles on their own cannot relieve poverty and social exclusion but they can be used to reduce the degradation and discrimination that accompany them. They therefore complement other social justice strategies such as socio-economic policies, equality rights and rights to fair treatment.

The rights provided for under the Human Rights Act are guaranteed to everyone, but there are people in our society who have particular need of human rights protection. These include those who are vulnerable, such as the elderly, the young and those with disabilities and health problems, particularly when they are resident in institutions. There are also many people who cannot access services or support and find themselves marginalised and discriminated against: homeless people; victims of crime; disabled people; lesbian, gay and bisexual people; black and minority ethnic people; transgendered people; refugees and asylum-seekers; and travellers and gypsies. Human rights principles, particularly the rights to life, to respect for private and family life and freedom from degrading treatment, are needed because they provide an enforceable system for protecting people when they experience maltreatment and discrimination.

The purpose of the human rights legislation, however, is not only to remedy injustices when they have occurred but also to act preventatively.

By providing a set of basic standards and requiring a positive approach from public authorities, the Act has the potential to transform the design and delivery of public services. It is intended do this by instilling a culture of respect for human rights within institutions providing such services and providing accountability when the standards are not met. The result should be an improvement in the quality of service provision and the benefits will accrue, not only to disadvantaged groups, but also to everyone who uses public services.

The focus so far has been on public authorities and how they approach their human rights responsibilities. Scant attention has been paid to empowering the largely forgotten beneficiaries to use the Human Rights Act to seek improvements in public services. The emphasis has been on the duty to provide rather than the right to receive. This is a missed opportunity because changes in society do not only happen from the top down.

How can individuals access their human rights effectively? Voluntary and community organisations exist to advance the interests of people experiencing disadvantage and discrimination: they could use human rights principles to negotiate changes in policy, practice and procedure. But our evidence reveals that many voluntary organisations working in the social justice field either do not see the relevance of the Act or have difficulty in using it in practice.

Two political developments in 2004, which stand in counterpoint to each other, provide a context for this report. In May, the Government published its proposals for establishing a Commission for Equality and Human Rights in 2007. The new Commission is designed to fill the gap in understanding and application of human rights principles to wider equality and social concerns and should achieve this in partnership with the voluntary and community sector. But the Human Rights Act is also now under political attack for allegedly contributing to a 'compensation culture' and benefiting the 'wrong people.' In August 2004, the Conservative Party announced that it has set up a commission to investigate the workings of the Act with a view to amending or repealing it. The question of how to apply the Human Rights Act more effectively for social justice purposes has now become urgent.

There are several reasons why the Human Rights Act is difficult for voluntary organisations working on social justice issues to use. The Act is based on the European Convention on Human Rights and neither is easy to understand nor to apply. Because the legislation also has an important function in realigning the constitutional relationship between the individual and the state, people have regarded its sole purpose as a legal tool to protect civil liberties. They also think that the Act can only be used in court cases and that, because of its poor reputation within the media and elsewhere as a last resort for unworthy causes, to use it would be counter-productive to the interests they seek to promote. The fact that the Human

Rights Act has been conflated with stories about 'ambulance-chasing' and that political capital can be made of this, demonstrates the lack of a common understanding of the positive contribution that human rights can make.

Since the Act came into force in 2000, the Government has failed to recognise the role that the voluntary and community sector could play in connecting human rights principles with social justice issues. Instead the emphasis has been on the liability that the Act could impose on voluntary organisations that provide public services on behalf of the statutory sector. Consequently, developments like the Compact between Government and the voluntary sector are not underpinned by human rights thinking.

What can the Human Rights Act add to existing strategies to advance the interests of their client groups? Most voluntary organisations consulted during this project stated a preference for using a rights-based approach to advance their clients' interests because of the opportunities it offers for empowerment and autonomy. These organisations recognised the conceptual link between the values that are fundamental to their work and human rights principles but are struggling to bridge the gap between theory and practice. Our research revealed that organisations are keen to explore practical ways that they could use the rights guaranteed by the Act to enhance what they are already doing, and to share these experiences with each other.

This report proposes a human rights framework that could be adopted and used by voluntary organisations. It amalgamates the principles of dignity, respect, equality, empowerment, participation and autonomy that underpin voluntary activity with the specific legal rights provided by the Human Rights Act. The framework is only a starting point because each organisation will have to consider its own priorities and seek relevant information about the legal rights applicable to its own concerns. The report does not attempt to provide such specialist information but has outlined some basic guidance on the rights protected by the Human Rights Act and recommended sources of further information in the appendices.

The proposition is that voluntary organisations should be able to use the Human Rights Act to hold government and other public authorities accountable for their obligations without having to resort to legal action. The Government forecast that the Act would provide the 'language you need to speak to win an argument' and this publication explores what happens or could happen when voluntary organisations use human rights language. There are a number of factors that create a favourable climate for voluntary sector engagement with human rights and these should constitute mechanisms of accountability. For example, it is helpful that the Human Rights Act tends to require public authorities to act positively to protect rights rather than merely negatively to avoid a breach because this allows room for preventative strategies. It is also helpful that the Audit

Commission and other inspectorates are increasingly using human rights principles to measure good practice within public authorities. Also, the Commission on Equality and Human Rights, when established, will be available to offer guidance and support to the voluntary and community sector in using human rights principles to achieve improvements in public services.

The consensus among voluntary organisations consulted during the project was to concentrate efforts on using human rights language with government and other public authorities. Not only do they have legal responsibilities under the Act but their approach to compliance should be in terms of institutional change. Large and specialist campaigning organisations operating nationally, however, report mixed experiences of using a human rights approach in their policy and campaigning work. The report refers to some of these experiences in relation to negotiation with government officials, briefings to parliament and public campaigns. The Government needs to adopt a more consistent approach both to its own compliance with the Human Rights Act and to implementing the United Nations and other human rights instruments as required by international law.

A majority of voluntary organisations operate at the local level and there is potential for many organisations, both large and small, to introduce human rights concepts into their work with regional and local public authorities. Many voluntary and community organisations, through advocacy and advice work, seek changes from social services departments, health trusts, housing authorities and schools on behalf of individuals. The Human Rights Act can be used to challenge practices and patterns of behaviour that adversely affect people using services but it can also be used to improve the quality of decisions as they are made. Development work done in collaboration with the public sector can influence procedure to prevent problems occurring in the first place as well as sorting them out when they have occurred. The report describes ways in which voluntary organisations have used and could use a human rights approach to improve procedure and practice within public authorities.

This publication concludes that the potential contribution that the Human Rights Act and its underlying principles could make to social justice is waiting to be realised. It argues that the voluntary and community sector, as a frequent intermediary between individuals using services and public authorities providing them, is in a prime position for using human rights as an agent of change. The publication therefore constitutes a call for action by the voluntary sector and its membership bodies. But first, voluntary and community organisations need practical and accessible information on what human rights are and what value they can add to their work on behalf of people experiencing disadvantage and discrimination. The report intends to invigorate that process and although it highlights the challenges involved, it also points to the way forward.

What else needs to be done? The Government passed the Human Rights Act but left unfinished the job of explaining what it was for and what it could do. The plan is for the new Commission on Equality and Human Rights to take on this work but it will not get going until seven years after the law came into effect. Progress needs to be made in the meantime. The Government has a responsibility to provide leadership and vision in promoting a common understanding of the association between the Human Rights Act and social justice questions. It needs also to provide practical guidance and support to voluntary and community organisations on what human rights are and what they can contribute to action on behalf of socially excluded and vulnerable people. If voluntary organisations receive useful information and substantial support on the applicability of the Human Rights Act, they will then be more able to implement a human rights approach in their policy and development work. If through using human rights language, voluntary organisations go on to find that they are able to effect improvements in the design of policy and procedure and changes in day-to-day practice, then the question of who needs human rights will have been answered.

Introduction

Expectations were raised when the Human Rights Act was passed. The UK would have a bill of rights that guaranteed the fundamentals for a civilised society based on mutual respect and regard for dignity. New legal responsibilities on public authorities constituted the means for encouraging a cultural change that would improve the provision of public services and consequently the treatment of and respect for socially excluded and deprived people. The introduction of positive legal rights would ensure accountability when they were breached.

But evidence has revealed both the failure of public authorities to connect compliance with the Human Rights Act with improvements in public services, and the mal-treatment of marginalised and vulnerable service users (Joint Committee on Human Rights (JCHR), 2003; Audit Commission, 2003; British Institute of Human Rights (BIHR), 2002). The result is that the Act has hardly benefited the people who have the most need of its protection. This has happened because, apart from optimistic statements from the Government when the law was passed, there has been an absence of leadership and support to ensure that these objectives can be achieved. Instead, the impact of the Act has been mainly in the courtroom and the popular perception is that human rights are either not relevant in wider society or are applied to unworthy causes. The Human Rights Act is now under attack politically. The Conservative Party has set up a commission to review the Act and to consider whether it should be repealed because the 'wrong people' have used it to their advantage.

The question that urgently needs to be answered is how can the principles of the Human Rights Act be applied for the benefit of vulnerable individuals experiencing poor treatment, discrimination and social exclusion? It is unlikely that they will be able to access their human rights effectively on their own but will need support to do so. The voluntary and community sector exists to further their interests and many voluntary organisations have the capacity to seek changes from public authorities on their behalf without necessarily having to go to court. But do they use the Human Rights Act in their work? If not, then how could they so that it can be applied for the purposes for which it was intended?

This report examines the engagement with human rights among voluntary organisations working to advance the interests of vulnerable and socially excluded people. Its purpose is to achieve three principal objectives. Firstly, to show how human rights principles have practical application to the work of the voluntary sector on social justice issues. Secondly to demonstrate ways in which human rights can be used by the voluntary sector to further the interests of the people whom they represent. Thirdly, to illustrate methods of holding government and other public authorities accountable for their human rights obligations without resorting to litigation. Our suggestions on these questions are not intended to be definitive but to encourage further consideration and debate.

The Government is establishing a Commission for Equality and Human Rights in 2007. One function of the new Commission will be to help give specificity to public authorities in understanding their responsibilities under the Act. In the long-term this should ensure better protection of people's human rights. The Commission will need to work closely with voluntary and community organisations in progressing this work because, where they represent users, they play an important role at the local level in encouraging service providers to meet their legal obligations. This research is also intended to make a contribution to the development of that work.

Structure

This publication has been divided into the two parts that reflect its title. Part 1 considers what human rights are and why they are needed and Part 2 addresses the ways in which the voluntary sector can use human rights.

The report starts by outlining the legal sources of human rights in the UK, concentrating on the Human Rights Act and the European Convention on Human Rights on which the Act is based but referring also to the international human rights treaties. The first chapter emphasises the application of Convention rights to social justice issues. Chapter 2 outlines the underlying principles of the Act and explores how the Act fits in with existing laws, policies and strategies on social justice. Many voluntary organisations, however, do not use the Human Rights Act and the next chapter explores the reasons why. Chapter 4 pulls together the common themes and proposes a framework for human rights.

The opening chapter in Part 2 considers the role of the voluntary sector and identifies possible mechanisms that can be used to hold public authorities accountable for their human rights responsibilities. Chapter 6 goes on to consider general points about implementation of a rights-based approach. The remaining chapters of the report consider ways in which voluntary organisations use or could use human rights in practice and what the experiences have been so far. This inquiry is done by reference in Chapter 7 to influencing policy at the national level through work with government, parliament, test case litigation and public campaigns. Chapter 8 explores ways to use human rights to change procedure and practice at the local level both through work on preventing problems arising as well as sorting them out when they have occurred. Conclusions and recommendations are contained in Chapter 9.

Scope and methodology

Our research considered the application of human rights principles to social justice concerns particularly in relation to improving public services outside a litigation context. We included within our remit voluntary organisations in England and Wales, which support people in the following groups where they experience discrimination and disadvantage: children and young people, disabled people, homeless and poorly housed people, black and minority ethnic groups, older people, lesbian, gay and bisexual people, people with mental health problems, people in poverty, refugees and asylum-seekers, religious minorities, transgendered people, travellers and gypsies, victims of crime and women. We did not include work done by voluntary organisations on behalf of people accused or convicted of crimes or on behalf of prisoners. Because of our focus on public services, employment rights were also excluded.

We held seminars in London and Newcastle attended by large and medium-size NGOs, voluntary membership organisations and coalitions, public authorities, inspectorates, academics and human rights experts. We obtained responses to a questionnaire from thirty voluntary organisations ranging in size from those with fewer than ten staff members to those with over a hundred employees and we also conducted individual interviews. Overall we have obtained the views of about sixty voluntary organisations on which we base the findings in this report.

Section 1

Human rights: what are they
and why do we need them?

1 Legal sources of human rights in the UK

This chapter outlines the legal basis for human rights in the UK. It is principally concerned with the Human Rights Act which introduced the rights and freedoms guaranteed by the European Convention on Human Rights (ECHR). The ways in which the Convention rights can affect domestic law, policy-making and the delivery of public services are outlined. The chapter also briefly considers the United Nations covenants and other international instruments because the government has treaty obligations to implement their provisions in the UK. In keeping with this publication's focus on social justice issues arising from the design and delivery of public services, the discussion concentrates on the human rights provisions that are relevant to those matters.

The European Convention on Human Rights

The European Convention on Human Rights is a treaty of the forty-five member countries of the Council of Europe (a political organisation entirely separate from the European Union). The Convention constitutes a regional arrangement reflecting particularly the civil and political rights of the Universal Declaration of Human Rights of 1948. British Foreign Office lawyers were involved in drafting the Convention and it was ratified by the UK in 1951.

The rights protected by the Convention include the right to life, liberty, fair hearing, private and family life, freedom of thought, conscience and religion, free expression, free association, freedom from degrading treatment, access to education, enjoyment of possessions and freedom from discrimination in enjoyment of Convention rights. Some of the Convention rights, like the right to life and freedom from degrading treatment are 'absolute', while others like the right to private and family life are 'qualified'. Qualified rights may be restricted on specified grounds and in particular circumstances. Under the principle of 'proportionality', the qualified rights of individuals and groups may need to be considered in the context of the rights and interests of other individuals as well as the wider community and any restrictions imposed on people's rights must be the minimum needed to strike a fair balance. So, for example, the right to free expression can be restricted by laws preventing incitement to racial hatred.

The purpose of this publication is not to educate the reader on the ambit of ECHR rights or the court cases that have been decided in relation to them. But in recognition of the fact that some guidance might be useful, a brief and selective summary of the Convention rights and how they have been applied in practice is provided in the appendix. The guide in the appendix is only a starting point and it does not claim to be comprehensive. What has been evident throughout our research is the unmet need within voluntary organisations for practical information on the Convention rights, what they apply to and how they can be used. This publication cannot fulfil that function because each voluntary organisation will have different needs and priorities. The intention is to highlight what information does need to be provided.

Individuals have the right to apply to the European Court of Human Rights, sitting in Strasbourg on the grounds that member states have failed to comply with the Convention. The Strasbourg Court has made several significant judgements finding UK law and governmental policy in breach of the Convention (see appendix).

The Human Rights Act

The source of legally enforceable human rights in the UK is the Human Rights Act 1998. The Act, which came into force in 2000, incorporated the rights guaranteed under the European Convention on Human Rights into UK law. This process effectively, in the present Government's words, 'brought rights home' to the British people. Prior to the Act, remedies under the ECHR had only been available upon direct application to the European Court of Human Rights. The position now is that applications can be made to the Strasbourg court after they have been considered by UK courts.

By domesticating the ECHR, legal liability was extended beyond central government to all 'public authorities'. These include local authorities, health authorities and health trusts, schools, courts, tribunals, police, prisons and any non-statutory organisation exercising a 'public function' (Parliament, however, is excluded). The Act requires public authorities to act 'compatibly' with Convention rights (section 6) and provides a right for a 'victim' to bring legal proceedings in UK courts against a public authority for breach of Convention rights or raise a Convention right argument in any existing proceedings (section 7). The Act also sets out the way in which courts should apply the Convention rights to existing laws.

The European Court of Human Rights continues to have an effect on UK court decisions and government policy-making in two ways. Firstly, by hearing applications brought against the UK government and secondly, because of the way in which it keeps the ECHR articles under review. This means that what the Strasbourg Court has said about the meaning of the Convention (even in cases that do not involve the UK) is as important as the wording of the articles themselves.

The application of Convention rights

As the following examples show, although the European Convention on Human Rights is primarily concerned with civil and political rights, it reaches across the social policy field. The Human Rights Act affects the way in which public services are provided in practice as well as how law, policy and procedure are developed in relation to those services. This means that the requirement to think about Convention rights is not confined to policy-makers and senior managers setting procedures but also to all members of staff who are engaged in providing services directly to users. It also means that voluntary and community organisations need to comprehend the potential breadth of the Act, not just in terms of the wide range of services affected but also in relation to how they are delivered.

The effect on UK laws

The Human Rights Act has an effect on legislation in three express ways. Firstly, when introducing bills, the Government must state whether it thinks they are compliant with the Convention (section 19). Parliament retains the power to pass laws that are not compatible with Convention rights but the Strasbourg court system remains available for challenging UK state action in breach of the Convention. Secondly, the Act has an effect on the judicial interpretation of domestic laws. Courts must 'read' legislation, as far as possible, in line with Convention rights (section 3). The consequence has been, for example, that same-sex couples now have the right to succeed to a tenancy following the death of a partner. The House of Lords interpreted references to 'living together as husband and wife' in the Rent Act 1977 as including the requirement not to discriminate on grounds of sexual orientation (*Ghaidan* case, 2004).

Thirdly, where the UK courts find it impossible to 'read' the Convention rights into the relevant law, they can make 'declarations of incompatibility' (section 4). This happened with the provision in the Mental Health Act requiring patients detained in hospital to prove that they no longer suffered mental illness before they could be discharged. The Court held that this breached patients' right to liberty (Article 5) and the Mental Health Act has been amended (*Mental Health RT* case, 2002).

The European Court of Human Rights can also apply Convention rights to fill a gap in UK law. For example, the Strasbourg court has recently held that detaining an autistic man without legal safeguards determining the circumstances of the detention was a breach of his right to liberty (Article 5(1)(4)) (*Bournewood* case, 2004).

Effect on policy and procedure

A range of health, social care, housing, planning, education and environmental policy decisions may involve human rights considerations. These issues can arise in policy-making at both national and local levels. For example, local authorities, when planning to close care homes for the elderly, must consider the rights of residents to respect for their private life and to their home (Article 8, *Madden* case, 2002). Another example is that nursing guidelines on the use of mechanical lifting devices in place of manual handling must take into account the need to respect the dignity of the patient as well as the safety of the medical professional (*East Sussex* case, 2003).

Other examples where Convention rights are likely to apply include: the disclosure of personal information (right to private and family life, Article 8), the use of 'Do Not Resuscitate' notices (right to life, Article 2), discrimination in healthcare provision – often called the 'postcode lottery' – (Articles 2 and 14), identity and other issues relating to gender reassignment (right to private and family life, right to marry, Articles 8 and 12), rehousing and other protection for victims of crime (right to private and family life, possibly right to life, Articles 2 and 8), school exclusions (right to education, Protocol 1, Article 2), banning the hijab headscarf in public authority buildings (right to religious freedom and non-discrimination, Articles 9 and 14), lack of accommodation and other facilities for travellers and gypsies (Articles 8 and 14) and environmental pollution (Article 8).

Effect on practical delivery of services

The legal requirement that public authorities act compatibly with Convention rights applies not only to the formulation of policy and procedure but implementation as well. This means that the Act applies both to the day-to-day decisions made by staff and to the way in which public services are provided. The purpose of the Act is to provide vulnerable service users with protection of their Convention rights but it has scarcely been used to prevent the numerous instances of poor treatment of such people. These have long been an unacceptable feature of our society and are a principal concern of the voluntary sector.

Some examples constitute cruelty and neglect and are an outrage to common decency. The *Daily Mirror*, earlier this year, published a number of instances gathered by Action on Elder Abuse about the appalling treatment of older people. Many of the cases deserved criminal prosecution. An elderly woman had her fingernails torn out, other people died of hypothermia after being left by open windows. There are many other instances of maltreatment and abuse that may never be considered in a court but are shameful nonetheless and constitute a failure to protect people's human rights. There is a concern, however, that even if such cases were brought to court, legal liability might not be established. A report by the British Institute of Human Rights revealed that care home residents were given their breakfast while sitting on the toilet (BIHR, 2002). In a recent speech, Brenda Hale, the House of Lords judge observed that such practice seemed to her to be an obvious human rights abuse although she wondered whether it would seem obvious to the law (Hale, 2004).

Other examples where Convention rights will apply to the way in which public services are delivered include: the use of baffle locks and medication to subdue residents within institutions for the elderly and mentally ill (Articles 5 and 8), making elderly residents wear incontinence pads, even though they are not incontinent (Articles 3 and 8), leaving patients on trolleys in corridors (Articles 3 and 8), inappropriate and insensitive treatment of women alleging rape and other violence (Article 8), preventing someone from wearing a hat in court following chemotherapy (Article 8) and the consequences of poor housing conditions (Articles 3 and 8).

Positive obligations

The European Convention on Human Rights imposes requirements on member states to 'secure' Convention rights to 'everyone within their jurisdiction' (Article 1). The European Court has interpreted this article to mean that states have 'positive obligations' to protect Convention rights. For example, legal processes need to be available to ensure that Convention rights can be protected. The Strasbourg court criticised the defence of reasonable chastisement under UK law as insufficiently protecting children from degrading treatment (*A v. UK*, 1999). In certain circumstances, public authorities may need to take positive action even where the complaint is against private persons. For example, four siblings successfully applied to the Strasbourg Court on the grounds that Bedfordshire County Council had not protected them from their parents' abuse and neglect – Social Services had failed to place the children on the Child Protection Register – (*Bedfordshire CC case*, 2002).

The effect of the 'positive obligations' principle under the Human Rights Act is that public authorities in the UK may need to adopt a proactive rather than passive approach to ensuring that they act compatibly with Convention rights. Other instances where this doctrine could apply include the problems of infant mortality in the travelling population, bullying in schools and protecting victims of crime. The principle is important in understanding the nature and extent of legal responsibilities on public authorities although the courts are developing it cautiously. It also forms the legal basis for the Government's stated commitment to develop a culture of respect for human rights, discussed below.

Resources

There are situations where the Human Rights Act may require changes in policies and practices, which will involve the allocation of resources and costs. For example, the need to avoid discrimination in the healthcare provided to patients based on age or locality (right to life) or the education of children with special needs (right to education) may have cost implications.

In some cases, these could be considerable. For example, provision of expensive life-saving treatment will engage the right to life of the affected patients but at the risk of compromising spending in other areas of the health service. Immediate pressures on resources need to be balanced, however, against future savings and returns gained from early investment in, staying with these examples, healthcare and education. The issue of the costs to government and other public authorities of providing substantive services to the extent they may be required by the Human Rights Act (as opposed to training on human rights implementation) is outside the remit of this publication but it clearly deserves consideration.

International human rights instruments

The other legal bases for human rights in the UK are derived from international treaties and the obligations that they impose on member state signatories. For example, the European Union Constitution, signed on 29 October 2004, contains a Charter of Fundamental Rights. If the Constitution is ratified, the Charter is likely to have a significant impact on the domestic socio-economic sphere. The UK has also ratified other treaties of the Council of Europe such as the European Social Charter (though not the revised charter).

The principal international human rights instruments are the United Nations covenants, which are legally binding as treaties on the member states that are parties to them. They set standards for protection of human rights and provide measures for domestic implementation. In particular, there are UN covenants protecting civil and political rights, and economic, social and cultural rights and against torture and degrading treatment. There are also covenants that aim to eliminate racial discrimination, discrimination against women and to protect the rights of children.

The UK has ratified but not incorporated the UN covenants into UK law so individuals cannot rely on them to obtain legal remedies. Governments have also been reluctant to sign up to mechanisms that would allow individuals to complain directly to the United Nations committees that oversee implementation of the relevant covenants. But the government does have legal obligations to implement the provisions of the covenants within the UK, through law and policy. Some accountability is achieved through the UK courts, which have regard to the covenants on the assumption that governments intend to comply with their treaty obligations and by the compliance reviews undertaken by the Parliamentary Joint Committee on Human Rights (JCHR, 2003 and 2004).

UN procedures require the government of the day to report periodically on implementation measures, which are then scrutinised by the relevant UN committee. This process provides an opportunity, which is taken up by many of the larger voluntary and specialist organisations to seek to hold the government accountable for the UK's treaty obligations and to encourage public authorities to adopt the principles of the covenants as measures of best practice. Groups working on behalf of children and young people have made substantial progress in increasing governmental compliance with the UN Convention on the Rights of the Child particularly in relation to participation by children in decisions that affect them and in establishing children's commissioners in the four nations of the UK. There has been less success, however, with encouraging government to implement the UN covenant on economic, social and cultural rights and the reasons for this are outlined in the next chapter.

The international treaties are potentially important tools for the voluntary sector but work on implementing them in the UK tends to be confined to specialist NGOs. Since this report concentrates on the Human Rights Act and because familiarity with the UN covenants and procedures for enforcing them is at the advanced level for the average voluntary organisation, they will not be given the attention here that they deserve but their significance should not be underplayed.

2 Why human rights are needed

The exposition so far has been of the practical application of the Human Rights Act and international instruments to pressing social problems. The examples referred to in the previous chapter demonstrate the utility of human rights principles in remedying the injustices that accompany such problems. The function of the Human Rights Act is, however, to achieve more than relief from injustice in particular cases. As the underlying principles confirm, its purpose is to be transformative by encouraging changes to be made that will prevent injustices from occurring. How does this piece of progressive legislation fit in with existing laws, policies and strategies that address social justice questions?

A human rights culture

Before the Act came into force, the Government emphasised that the legislation was intended to do more than create new opportunities for litigation. Jack Straw MP, then Home Secretary, anticipated that the Act would lead to a cultural change within public services because it represented 'the ethical bottom line for public authorities...a fairness guarantee for the citizen' which should 'help build greater confidence in our public authorities'. Lord Irvine, then Lord Chancellor explained it in the following way:

> What I mean and I am sure what others mean when they talk of a culture of respect for human rights is to create a society in which our public institutions are habitually, automatically responsive to human rights considerations in relation to every procedure they follow, in relation to every practice they follow, in relation to every decision they take, in relation to every piece of legislation they sponsor (Irvine, 2001).

By creating a framework within which public policy and practice is determined, the Act is designed to work preventatively. The consequences for public services are intended to be transformational.

The Home Secretary also envisaged that the Act would transform the nation's culture because it provided:

> an ethical language we can all recognise and sign up to, a...language which doesn't belong to any particular group or creed but to all of us. One that is based on principles of common humanity (Straw, 1999).

This ethical language was essential to learn because it would be 'the language you need to speak to win an argument' (Straw, 1999). Commentators also saw the potential that a UK bill of rights offered to promote a coalition of shared values in a dystopian world. Leading human rights expert, Francesca Klug saw the Act as establishing a framework:

> which emphasises tolerance, privacy and autonomy on the one hand, and concern for the rights of others and the needs of the wider community on the other (Klug, 2000).

The effect of introducing the Human Rights Act was to change the basis on which people's human rights could be regarded. The Parliamentary Joint Committee on Human Rights expressed it as follows:

> Citizens enjoy certain rights as an affirmation of their equal dignity and worth, and not as a contingent gift of the state (JCHR, 6th report, 2003).

These conceptions of human rights derive from the Universal Declaration of Human Rights 1948, which was founded on the principles of dignity and respect and desire for social progress as well as functioning as a mechanism to prevent atrocities committed by tyrannical regimes. The Declaration was based on a recognition of 'the importance of social justice and human rights as the foundation for a stable international order' (Brownlie, 1994) and is expressed in the preamble as follows:

> Whereas, the peoples of the United Nations have in the Charter reaffirmed their faith in fundamental human rights, in the inherent dignity and worth of the human person and in the equal rights of men and women and have determined to promote social progress and better standards of life in larger freedom.

United Nations member states have 'pledged themselves to achieve the promotion of universal respect for and observance of human rights and fundamental freedoms' which requires 'a common understanding' for the pledge to be fully realised.

If the philosophical connection between human rights principles and fundamental values for a socially just society can be made, there must be potential for the former to assist in progressing the latter. Voluntary sector respondents to our questionnaire overwhelmingly agreed that 'human rights are 'something for everyone' and should be capable of being used outside a courtroom to promote social justice.' The problem is how to move from stirring rhetoric to practical application.

Social justice

The notion of 'social justice' is based on the recognition of the equal worth of all citizens. It requires the empowerment and autonomy of individuals and their communities, the alleviation of poverty, the achievement of social inclusion and the elimination of unjust inequalities. These concepts are evaluated in social terms founded on principles of common humanity and the desire for a just society but their achievement has economic consequences. Progress towards greater equality requires the distribution of state resources, which are intended to relieve poverty and social exclusion, ensure that basic financial needs are met and that equal opportunities are realised.

How do the human rights principles provided by the Human Rights Act and the international treaties fit in with existing laws and policies on social justice questions? What can these principles contribute to existing strategies for pursuing the interests of vulnerable and socially excluded people? The concept of 'human rights' may be new in the UK but the concept of 'rights' in social justice terms is not. The social policy reforms of the 1940s and the creation of the welfare state provided rights to healthcare, education, housing and benefits as attributes of citizenship. Other long-standing social rights reforms include the acts targeting discrimination against women and against people of different races and more recently against disabled people. Achieving greater participation and empowerment for marginalised and vulnerable people are also well-established social justice goals.

The Human Rights Act

Apart from the right of access to education and the right to peaceful enjoyment of possessions, the Human Rights Act does not guarantee substantive socio-economic rights. Instead, by setting out the rights to which human beings are entitled by virtue of their humanity (as opposed to their citizenship), the Act guarantees certain standards affecting the way in which public services are provided or state assets distributed. As has been described, this includes policy-making and procedure as well as practice. It may, on occasion, lead to requirements that substantive services be provided. The decision of the Court of Appeal in May 2004 in favour of destitute asylum-seekers that 'shelter of some form from the elements at night' is a 'basic amenity' has the effect of applying human rights principles (freedom from inhuman and degrading treatment, Article 3) to certain instances of homelessness, although in the UK there is no legally enforceable 'human right' to housing (*Limbuela* case, 2004).

The relationship between social justice and the Human Rights Act is, therefore, arguably one based on consequences. Poverty and socio-economic deprivation do not in the UK constitute human rights violations but the consequential social exclusion, discrimination and degradation experienced by those in poverty do engage human rights considerations. In Convention rights terms, these involve the enforceable legal rights to life, liberty, private and family life and freedom from degrading treatment and discrimination. Oxfam, for example, characterises poverty in the UK as a 'denial of human rights' but the approach implies that it is the inferior and degrading conditions in which people in poverty find themselves that constitute the denial of human rights (and potentially provide the legal remedy for such denial) (Oxfam, 2001).

Socio-economic rights

The objective of the International Covenant on Economic, Social and Cultural Rights (ICESCR) is the achievement of social justice through socio-economic means and the UN Committee that supervises its implementation has emphasised that poverty does constitute a denial of human rights under the Covenant (CESCR, 2001). The Covenant provides for the 'right of everyone' to an 'adequate standard of living (including the right to food, clothing and housing)', the 'enjoyment of the highest attainable standard of physical and mental health', the right to work, social security and education (Articles 11, 12, 6, 9 and 13). Furthermore, the UK government as a signatory is required to 'take steps...to the maximum of its available resources' to achieve 'progressively the full realization' of these specified rights (Article 2).

Because the covenant envisages an incremental approach, successive governments have, however, tended to regard socio-economic rights more as aspirational policy objectives than legal obligations under international law. Socio-economic questions are also still regarded domestically within a welfare or social policy paradigm rather than in rights-based terms. Voluntary sector campaigners have struggled to find ways to hold government accountable for implementing socio-economic rights under the Covenant because of arguments about how to prioritise the resources that will need to be applied. It was not surprising that most of the respondents to the questionnaire said that they did not refer to the Covenant in their work.

Greater progress in promoting socio-economic rights, however, has been made in Northern Ireland where such rights are seen to be a unifying factor among divided communities (Beirne, 2004). There are useful lessons to be learned from the Northern Ireland experience as well as opportunities to build on the support that socio-economic rights (such as healthcare and housing) enjoy among the general public (State of the Nation, 2000). The most significant development in this field is the recent report on the ICESCR of the Parliamentary Joint Committee on Human Rights (JCHR, 2004). By expressing the view that 'a rights-based approach can assist government in addressing poverty,' the parliamentary Committee has made it clear that social justice policies should be considered within a socio-economic rights framework. The Committee proposes several measures to achieve greater accountability by government and increased participation by the voluntary sector in realising fuller implementation of socio-economic rights in the UK.

Rights to equality

The right to equal treatment and freedom from discrimination are fundamental human rights. Traditionally, in the UK, however, equality has not been seen as a human rights issue and the campaigns for the rights of women, black and minority ethnic people, disabled people and lesbians and gays have in the past largely been fought on 'equal rights' rather than 'human rights' terms. Although the sex, race and disability legislation is expressed in 'black letter law' terms outlawing discriminatory acts rather than promoting equal rights, the equality movements are firmly rights-based. Human rights arguments are increasingly being used by equality organisations. One such group campaigning for transgender rights commented, 'we flip flop between arguments based on equal rights and human rights.'

The Human Rights Act was welcomed by equality campaigners although the ECHR is weak in respect of equality rights. Article 14 is not a free-standing human right but only applies in relation to discrimination in the 'enjoyment' of the other Convention rights. Protocol 12 to the Convention provides a substantive right to equality but it has not been signed or ratified by the UK and so is not part of domestic human rights and equalities law. Voluntary organisations working in those fields have also recognised the applicability of the UN covenants on gender and race (CEDAW and CERD) and used them in their policy work.

Our questionnaire sought to compare and contrast the Human Rights Act with the anti-discrimination legislation. Twenty-five of the thirty organisations responding said that they used one or more of the Sex Discrimination Act, Race Relations Act and Disability Discrimination Act in their work. Thirteen organisations agreed with the statement that discrimination laws are 'easier to use than the Human Rights Act', although three said they were not, and another thirteen said they did not know. We pursued some theories on this, inviting responses. Two-thirds of those replying agreed that: 'discrimination laws are better targeted at the problems whereas the Human Rights Act is too broad and vague.' Slightly more people agreed that discrimination laws are: 'better understood because they have been around for longer,' and three-quarters agreed that 'better guidance exists as to how to use discrimination legislation' and that 'the discrimination laws already have Commissions to back them up.'

Human rights principles can assist the promotion of equality and social inclusion because they apply to everyone whereas anti-discrimination legislation applies only to particular groups. Human rights are particularly significant in legal challenges relating to ill-treatment of groups of people when, reportedly, the so-called 'bastard defence' is threatened. This suggests that there is no discrimination (and therefore no liability under relevant legislation) because everyone in the group is treated equally badly.

The increasing convergence between human rights and equality is exemplified by the recent legislative developments on equality. The statutory duty to promote good relations between different racial and ethnic groups contained in the Race Relations (Amendment) Act 2000 is being complemented by similar duties on public authorities to provide equal opportunities for disabled people and for women. Positive duties shift the emphasis from tackling specific instances of discrimination towards realising the goal of equality. By requiring institutional change, these new equality laws have a transformative and preventative purpose that is comparable to the positive obligations doctrine contained in the human rights legislation. The work being done in advance of setting up the Commission on Equality and Human Rights is encouraging a closer examination of the relationship and interaction between human rights and equality.

Rights to fair treatment

Human rights, particularly the right to a fair trial but also the underlying principles of dignity and respect, complement work done in the UK on fair treatment in access to public services. These are founded on concepts of autonomy and empowerment for service users and include matters like:

- accurate and accessible information being provided;

- consultation and participation;

- advocacy opportunities;

- fair decisions;

- reasons for decisions being given;

- reasons for refusal being relevant;

- right to appeal or redress.

During the 1990s (before the Human Rights Act), ippr considered the question of using these types of procedural rights to improve public services. A study into practical ways of 'developing new rights for people seeking health or social care' reported the convergence of several trends:

> [T]he idea of rights within public services has gained ground with the shift in Welfare State philosophy away from paternalism and towards autonomy, independence and social participation; with the new consumerism manifested in the Citizen's Charter; a new trend towards judicial interventionism; new roles for public audit and inspection; and problems of scarcity and rationing. (Bynoe, 1997)

The conclusion was that rights to fair treatment 'help to promote publicly accountable organisations and just dealing between citizens' although one of the main barriers identified was 'the unfamiliarity of most organisations with the concept of rights' (Bynoe, 1997). The Human Rights Act, by introducing a new 'concept of rights' provides a statutory and therefore authoritative basis to initiatives to improve fair treatment in public services.

Rights-based approaches in international development

Rights-based approaches, in which socio-economic progress is founded on human rights principles, are well-established in international development programmes. The Department for International Development (DFID), for example, has identified the following trends emerging in the last ten years:

> The development of 'rights-based' approaches as a means of:
>
> - Empowering people to exercise their 'voice', and so acquire immediate benefits but also influence processes of change and social transformation.
>
> - Helping the state to clarify its responsibilities towards citizens, in terms of respecting, protecting, promoting or fulfilling rights ...
>
> - Helping to translate the lofty principles of international declarations and conventions into practice (DFID, 2004).

International NGOs have adopted this approach in development programmes. For example, Oxfam is seeking to apply rights-based thinking across all areas of policy and practice. An internal paper describes it as including:

> Building human rights into programme design (e.g. by focusing programme goals on people and their rights; strengthening the accountability of duty bearers for human rights; supporting people to demand their rights; fighting discrimination and promoting equality and inclusion in policies, services and programmes; working with other agencies towards common rights-based goals); and
>
> Promoting rights-based policy and practice changes (e.g. by ensuring adequate progress and provision of effective remedies; ensuring laws and policies embody rights principles; allocating resources and budgets equitably; encouraging participation so that people can claim their rights; building social norms, attitudes and behaviours; ensuring quality of institutions and institutional capacity; basing economic policies on human rights).

Working methods of this sort founded on 'human rights' are usually absent from domestic policy-making and discourse, although elements like participation, accountability and empowerment are frequently deployed. The approach of UK governments has largely been that human rights are something that other countries need to comply with and aid has been provided to encourage them to do so. But there is little if any acknowledgement within government that the work that DFID is doing has any comparable relevance in a domestic context. The UK is under a legal obligation to comply with the UN treaties but there is no suggestion that DFID should share its expertise with other departments in Whitehall to 'help translate the lofty principles of international declarations and conventions into practice' in a domestic context. The Department for Constitutional Affairs (DCA) has recently completed an inter-departmental review of the UK's position in relation to international human rights instruments. It lists all the legal commitments to which the UK is subject but it does not address implementation measures at all (DCA, 2004).

The principles underlying rights-based approaches used abroad, which are outlined above are clearly of relevance in the UK and in harmony with the principles underlying the Human Rights Act, yet this connection is scarcely recognised or pursued in government or policy-making circles. In particular, the relevance of human rights to poverty and social exclusion in the international context is clearly articulated in a way that it is not in the UK, despite the best efforts of organisations like Save the Children and Oxfam. While this Government in particular has a policy of encouraging the development of a culture of respect for human rights, there is an opportunity to use the international experience of applying rights-based approaches (available within government itself) in the UK context.

But, whether because of misunderstandings or lack of information about the Act, many voluntary organisations have not implemented a strategy reflecting human rights law and the social justice imperatives with which they are already engaged.

3 Challenges presented by the Human Rights Act

As many people have told us, there are several factors that make it difficult for the voluntary sector to use the Human Rights Act in their work. Some of these relate to how the Act is perceived and misperceived. Others relate to the nature of the Convention rights themselves and how they are thought to require legal determination. There is also the effect of the Act on the voluntary sector as service providers and the tendency within the sector towards increasing service provision on behalf of statutory authorities. In addition, the Government has not provided the support that the voluntary sector needs to be able to use the Human Rights Act. The consequence is that the Act is still not seen to be of much relevance or practical use.

Not widely used by the voluntary sector

The National Council for Voluntary Organisations and other organisations prepared briefings before the Act came into force, which recognised the potential that the Human Rights Act could offer to voluntary sector work (NCVO, 2000). But evidence reveals that this potential has been largely unrealised. Research carried out by the British Institute of Human Rights showed that 'many policy staff in voluntary organisations' did not see the Act as 'relevant to their work' (BIHR, 2002). Although we knew that several voluntary organisations have a good awareness of the Act, we wanted to find out what the wider picture was. We asked some national and regional voluntary sector umbrella organisations whether their members were using or requesting information about the Act:

> The answer to the question is clear: people are not using human rights. They don't know how to yet, there's no easy source of advice on it. How should this information be provided? Voluntary sector organisations are very small, they're not going to add something complex like this unless they get support.

> Our experience is that few organisations are using human rights as a tool. As a membership organisation ourselves we don't get requests for information on human rights.

> It's the same for us in Wales. We don't get requests for information on human rights.

Unsurprisingly, most respondents to the questionnaire tended to agree that, 'we haven't had enough information about the relevance of human rights' with a fifth agreeing with this 'strongly' but another fifth felt that they had received enough information. The consequence of inadequate information about the Human Rights Act led half the respondents to the questionnaire to agree that 'other legislation/frameworks are more useful' than the Act. Some voluntary organisations had clearly thought about the Human Rights Act and even had expectations that it would be useful but found it lacking. Someone working with adults with learning disabilities said:

> The Human Rights Act is the last tool that we would use. When it came out, we thought it sounded practical but in fact it hasn't turned out to be at all.

Another seminar participant put it more starkly:

> Human rights are complicated. They can be used in contradictory ways. For example, in child protection we are asked to consider the rights of abusers.

Another person attending the same seminar, who works as an advocate for particularly vulnerable people, felt that the idea of using human rights arguments was a far-fetched luxury:

> Human rights are like the icing on the cake for people who haven't got a cake or even bread and butter.

Perceptions of the Act

The Human Rights Act was introduced without a public debate that would have encouraged a common understanding of its purpose and relevance. As a consequence, at present, a number of interpretations of human rights are recognisable in British public discourse. The most established understanding of human rights is of a set of internationally agreed rules formulated after the horrors of two world wars, which are supposed to inhibit foreign despotic regimes from perpetrating torture, disappearances, extra-judicial killings and other atrocities against their own and neighbouring people. As a seminar participant summarised it:

> For most people, human rights means Amnesty and writing letters to Chile. We live in a liberal democracy where these rights are taken for granted.

Because these rights are 'taken for granted' in our society, for many people the need for the Human Rights Act was not evident and it was not clear what role it would play.

One appropriate and important place for the Act is to complement our civil liberties tradition. The effect of introducing positive and substantive rights, such as the right to liberty and freedom of expression, was to re-balance the constitutional relationship between the citizen and the state and tilt it, at least in theory, more in favour of the citizen. In practice, the

Human Rights Act has mostly been used to give further definition to the rights and freedoms of the individual in the face of state action restricting them. These fundamental rights have to be adjudicated in courts and often cause clashes between judges and government ministers. Several significant issues have been taken up by campaigning groups, like Liberty, and articulated on human rights grounds. Examples include the right to protest at the arms trade fair, whether detention centres for asylum-seekers infringe the right to liberty and more recently, the human rights consequences of detaining suspected foreign terrorists for prolonged periods without trial.

The British Institute of Human Rights operates an education and training programme, which raises awareness of human rights among voluntary and community groups in London and South East. In the last two years the programme has reached approximately three hundred organisations and the director summarised the position as follows:

> *Our experience is that human rights are not used at all. We come across an incredible lack of awareness of what human rights are about. People have not got the first idea at all. As part of our training sessions we ask people what human rights mean to them and the typical response is: disappearances and torture overseas or protecting the rights of terrorists or people like Myra Hindley. It seems that they have never had anyone raise human rights in any other contexts.*

These themes were followed up in the questionnaire. Responses were invited to the statement that 'human rights have more to do with civil liberties for individuals (freedom of speech, right to protest etc.) than with social justice issues for excluded groups.' Although nine out of twenty-seven organisations agreed (with two agreeing strongly) that this was the case, eighteen disagreed (of which ten disagreed strongly). A discrepancy between what people thought human rights meant and how it was felt that they were being interpreted was identified by one large organisation which 'disagreed strongly' that human rights 'have more to do with civil liberties' commenting 'although in practice, it tends to be played out in this way.'

There are other contexts in which human rights have been referred to. Celebrities like Naomi Campbell and Catherine Zeta Jones have used human rights arguments to help protect themselves from unwanted media intrusion. Their well-publicised court cases have encouraged a sense that human rights seem to be principally of interest to expensive lawyers. Some sections of the Press have also characterised the Human Rights Act as a 'criminal's charter' and the last refuge for unmeritorious defences.

The Conservative Party has recently announced the establishment of a commission to investigate the workings of the Act with a view to reforming or repealing it, which is due to report before the next election in 2005. Announcing the commission, the shadow Home Secretary, David Davis MP said:

The Human Rights Act has given rise to too many spurious rights. It has fuelled a compensation culture out of all sense of proportion and it is our aim to rebalance the rights culture.

The depth of opposition to human rights in some quarters should not be underestimated. An article in *The Spectator* suggested that:

considerations of people's supposed rights often paralyse sensible action [and] preclude kindness and common sense...they drive out considerations of...decency, tolerance [and] mutual obligation (*The Spectator*, 24.4.04).

In this interpretation of human rights, they seem to have become separated from morality. In fact, as shown above, human rights are founded on the principles of dignity and respect and do offer a framework for fundamental values. There is a consensus in our society about these values and a shared desire for social progress but a dissonance exists between those who believe that human rights can assist their achievement and those who believe that human rights will prevent it. The contested nature of human rights and the lack of any 'common understanding' within society of their value and purpose complicate their application to work undertaken by the voluntary sector.

Difficulties in using the Act

There are several reasons why the Human Rights Act and the accompanying Convention rights, are not easily understandable or accessible to voluntary and community groups and are therefore difficult to use. One is that what the voluntary sector needs to know about human rights is not available on the face of the legislation. Another is that it appears to be applicable mainly in legal proceedings. A third reason is that before it came into force, the Act appeared to be more likely to impose responsibilities on rather than create opportunities for the voluntary sector.

Convention rights: out-of-date, ill-defined and vague?
Many of the rights listed in the Convention seem quite arcane. 'Slavery' was abolished two hundred years ago and most voluntary groups working in the UK do not expect to come across instances of 'torture'. Other rights that might seem applicable, like the right to private and family life or the prohibition of degrading treatment are not defined in the statute and so it is not clear how they can be used. Respondents to the questionnaire were evenly split on the suggestion that the Convention rights are 'too vague' though several participants at seminars referred to problems in understanding the meaning of concepts like 'degrading' or 'inhuman'. Confusion was also expressed about the fact that some rights are absolute while others can be restricted and it is not clear what happens when rights conflict.

Traditionally the system of laws in the UK has been based on setting out the particulars of what is allowed and what is prohibited. In contrast, European legal traditions are based on codified frameworks and the European Convention on Human Rights is a creature of the latter tradition. The consequence is that a law providing a set of principles that is supposed to govern unspecified behaviour is unfamiliar in the UK and its reach is potentially so broad as to render it almost incomprehensible. In fact the Convention rights are being defined through cases heard by the European Court of Human Rights in Strasbourg and, since 2000, increasingly by the UK courts. Although the ramifications of court decisions are passed on to the public authorities which need to change their policies, there is insufficient dissemination to the voluntary sector of the principles on which those decisions were based and their wider implications.

In general, there are few people besides lawyers, human rights organisations and specialists who are familiar with how the courts have interpreted Convention rights and their consequential impact on the provision of public services, particularly on behalf of users. As a result, the literal wording of the Convention is as far as the average non-specialist will get and this encourages a sense that the Convention is out of date and lacking in relevance to modern concerns.

The Human Rights Act: mainly to be used in the courts?

The structure of the Human Rights Act is that it incorporates certain articles of the Convention (by listing them in a schedule) and provides a legal remedy for breach of Convention rights in the UK. It is therefore assumed by many people that a claim of human rights can only be made in connection with legal proceedings. Before the Act came into force, the Government concentrated on training the judiciary and this has reinforced the sense that the primary purpose of the Act is to provide redress through the courts.

Information provided from governmental sources emphasises the legalistic nature of the Act. The Government is right to provide people with information on how to access legal remedies under the Act and there is a legal basis for it too. The Government is under an obligation to comply with Article 13 of the ECHR, which requires member states to provide their citizens with 'an effective remedy before a national authority.' Article 13 is not incorporated into UK law because the Human Rights Act itself is designed to provide the remedy. This has led to a sense that provision of legal remedies is the Act's principal function and that the burden of enforcing the Human Rights Act is on the individual 'victim' through legal proceedings. The Community Legal Service leaflet states:

> If you think a public authority has broken your Convention rights (or is going to), you can take court proceedings against them. You have

to show that you have been affected by what the public authority has done or is going to do (CLS, 2004).

There are difficulties for individuals in accessing legal remedies through the courts and the Government has not addressed alternative ways in which individuals can seek to enforce their rights. This is a missed opportunity and succeeding chapters explore ways in which the voluntary sector can contribute to such enforcement on behalf of particular groups of people. Most of the voluntary organisations responding to the questionnaire disagreed with the idea that 'human rights are only really applicable in legal cases' though one large organisation commented that this was the 'reality'. These responses seem to demonstrate the potential for expanding human rights protection beyond the courtroom, if practical means can be found.

Voluntary sector: potential liability under the Human Rights Act

When the Human Rights Act was passed the attention of voluntary organisations providing public services was less on the opportunities for using the Act than on the legal liability that it potentially imposed. Pressure to comply with the Act without any confirmation that it would apply, dominated voluntary sector thinking about the Act before it came into force. As has been described, the Act requires compliance from 'public authorities'. This term is defined to include any organisation that has 'functions of a public nature' (section 6(3)(b)). If a charity is providing services such as residential homes or social housing, do these constitute 'public functions' and thereby classify the charity as a 'public authority' with responsibilities under the Act?

The information provided by the Government before the Act came into force and since has focused on the voluntary sector as service providers because of this potential liability. In 2000, the Home Office, Human Rights Unit produced a leaflet which offered speculative examples, based on ministerial statements during the bill's passage through Parliament, of the sorts of organisations which might have legal responsibilities. These included:

> some charities and other voluntary organisations which carry out public functions for or instead of central or local authorities. This could include running residential homes (Home Office, 2000).

A number of court judgements have, however, narrowed the definition of 'public authority' in a way not intended by Parliament and made it more complicated to understand and apply. In one case, a housing association providing rented accommodation on behalf of a local authority was held to be a public authority (*Poplar Housing*, 2001). In another case, a private provider of mental health care was also held to be a public authority in relation to a claim by a patient whose care was financed by her health authority (*Partnerships in Care*, 2002). But in a third case, a voluntary sector care home provider was held not to be a public authority even though the residents' places were funded by their local authority (*Leonard Cheshire*, 2002). In that case, the Leonard Cheshire Foundation was responding to a challenge under Article 8 (right to respect for private life and home) by residents of a care home that it was intending to close.

The complication is that the courts have laid down a series of tests to be applied in determining whether a non-statutory service provider will be a public authority. These tests look not only at the function being provided to see how 'public' it is, but also at the nature and proximity of the relationship between the private provider and the commissioning statutory authority. The emphasis on the institutional arrangements risks undermining the purpose of the Act, which is to provide protection of Convention rights. The Parliamentary Joint Committee on Human Rights described the effect of these tests 'in human rights terms, [as] highly problematic' because:

> the protection of human rights is dependent not on the type of power being exercised, nor on its capacity to interfere with human rights, but on the relatively arbitrary (in human rights terms) criterion of the body's administrative links with institutions of the State (JCHR, 7th report, 2004).

As a consequence, the law unfairly discriminates between users of services, like residents of care homes, who are similarly situated and receiving the same services but who enjoy different legal entitlements in relation to those services. Individuals seeking redress will have to overcome the hurdle of attributing responsibility before their claim under the Act can be considered. The problem is made worse by increasing private and voluntary sector provision of public services.

For the purposes of this report, use of the term 'public authority' is based on the current ambiguous definition, which may include voluntary sector providers particularly where they are contracted to statutory authorities. The effect of the potential liability issue is that large voluntary organisations, which provide a range of services, have tended to regard the Human Rights Act as something to be complied with rather than as a tool to further the interests of their clients.

The voluntary sector's increasing focus on service provision

Current trends are encouraging a greater service provision role for the voluntary sector and this is also likely to affect how the sector regards its role in relation to human rights. It is a premise of this project that the voluntary sector plays a key role in influencing the political agenda and policy-making at a national level but also, at the local level, in representing individuals and groups in negotiations with public authorities to improve the services provided. Recent government initiatives to support the voluntary sector potentially affect this premise and raise questions about how effectively the voluntary sector can combine delivery and influencing functions. Questions affecting the future role of the voluntary sector in general fall outside the remit of this project but deserve consideration.

The recently established Futurebuilders fund of £125 million for infrastructure support and Changeup, the capacity building and infrastructure framework for the voluntary and community sector are likely to increase the role that the voluntary and community sector plays in the delivery of public services. A seminar participant from a leading disability organisation noted this trend commenting:

> One of the difficulties is that we are all so bogged down with doing the job of service provision that there's no time left for thinking about policy and campaigning.

Closer working relationships between government and the voluntary sector have implications for the way in which the latter pursue their objectives. The effect on using a rights-based approach has been identified:

> There is a reluctance to use the language of rights at the moment, not only in government but also in some parts of the voluntary sector. That's partly because the government is working increasingly in partnership with the voluntary sector, so the voluntary sector is rather reluctant to use that language if the government doesn't wish to, and they prefer the language of welfare and needs (BIHR, 2002).

The lack of government support to voluntary sector

Apart from guidance on the potential liability issue, the Government did not provide financial support or information to the voluntary sector about the Human Rights Act. As the head of policy at a leading advice agency observed at the time:

> We've all got the poster on the walls, but there's no one telling us what it means for the people that we represent.

Between 1998 and 2000, the Government spent £4.5 million on training the judiciary and other preparations for the Human Rights Act. Guidance was issued to both the statutory public sector and private and voluntary organisations providing public services about the legal responsibilities introduced by the Act. Although the Government emphasised that the Act was intended to encourage the development of a culture of respect for human rights, it did not expend resources on educating the voluntary sector on the role that it could play in achieving that objective.

In contrast, for example, the Department for Trade and Industry has recently made a total of nearly £2 million available over two years to support voluntary sector organisations in 'raising awareness and understanding of' and 'meeting the demand for information, advice and guidance on' the Employment Equality (sexual orientation and religion or belief) Regulations. This is expressed to be:

> in recognition that individuals and employers go to a wide range of organisations for information and advice on workplace issues - not just government sources (DTI, 2004).

There is a lack of connection between accountability for human rights and other initiatives being developed between government and the voluntary sector. For example, the Compact on Relations between Government and the Voluntary and Community Sector in England aims to improve partnership between the government and the voluntary sector, on the assumption that a strong voluntary sector is intrinsically beneficial to society. The Compact refers to the 'major and literally incalculable contribution' that voluntary and community organisations make to the development of society. In particular, they are seen as helping to 'alleviate poverty, improve the quality of life and involve the socially excluded.' The Compact recognises that voluntary organisations 'act as pathfinders for the involvement of users in the design and delivery of services and often act as advocates for those who have no voice. In doing so they promote both equality and diversity.' The Government has given the following undertaking to ensure this work can be effectively carried out:

> To recognise and support the independence of the sector, including its right within the law, to campaign, to comment on Government policy, and to challenge that policy, irrespective of any funding relationship that might exist (Home Office, 1998).

Since 2000, the Compact scheme has been extended to local government and to the work of local strategic partnerships. There is potential for the Compact to have far-reaching consequences at the regional and local level as well as with central government. But although the Compact refers to the importance of promoting equality of opportunity and is especially concerned with the interests and needs of excluded groups, such as people in the black and minority ethnic communities, there is no reference to the Human Rights Act or the development of a human rights culture in public services. As a consequence, partnership working between the public and voluntary sectors is not underpinned by human rights thinking and many opportunities for collaborative working on this issue have been missed.

The Government should make a substantive and visible connection between its support for the voluntary sector through the Compact and other initiatives (emanating from the Home Office, Active Communities Unit) and its encouragement of the public sector to develop a culture of respect for human rights (the work of the Human Rights Division at the

Department for Constitutional Affairs). The White Paper on the proposed equality and human rights commission notes that, in its relations with voluntary organisations, the new body will need to take the Compact into account (DTI, 2004). In order to fulfil its function to promote equality and human rights, the new Commission should pursue this issue and seek to make progress on it.

The Government lacked imagination in failing to recognise the role that the voluntary sector could have in using the Human Rights Act to further the interests of vulnerable client groups. The development of a human rights culture cannot be progressed just by supporting the public sector because changes in society do not happen only from the top down. The Joint Committee on Human Rights summarised the situation as follows:

> We applaud the work that had been done by the Audit Commission and others to encourage public authorities to absorb human rights thinking into the provision of public services. This will undoubtedly improve the quality of those services, which will benefit the people who use them, many of whom are vulnerable and marginalised. We are concerned, however, about the lack of awareness about human rights among voluntary sector organisations which represent the sort of people whom we believe the Human Rights Act is supposed to protect. The approach to building a culture of human rights needs to be bottom-up as well as top-down. There is little evidence that this is happening (JCHR, 11th report, 2004).

The question is how to engage the voluntary sector in the development of a human rights culture through their efforts on behalf of service users. It is to be hoped that the Commission on Equality and Human Rights will prioritise this work. A combination of a statutory duty to consult stakeholders and the possibility of grant funding being available for certain kinds of voluntary sector work may encourage effective partnership working between the Commission and the sector. But the immediate priority is for connections to be made between the Human Rights Act and the social justice questions which lie at the heart of voluntary sector concerns. These connections are addressed in the next chapter.

4 Designing a human rights framework

As this publication has intended to demonstrate, notwithstanding the challenges, the principles underlying the Human Rights Act do complement more general conceptions of social justice rights. They are also central to voluntary sector philosophies and should be able to make a substantive contribution to work undertaken by the sector. This chapter seeks to resolve the apparent disconnection between the Human Rights Act and underlying human rights principles by proposing a framework that is designed to be useful to voluntary organisations.

Common themes

The common themes of deprivation and injustice that are driving the social justice policies and strategies discussed here are:

- Lack of respect for people
- Disregard for people's dignity
- Discrimination
- Powerlessness
- Worthlessness

These issues are and always have been of concern to voluntary sector organisations representing people who experience these predicaments. What is new in the UK is that the Human Rights Act provides legal authority for challenging them. As a human rights expert observed:

> It's true that there are so many different standards but the human rights answer is that people need to be treated with dignity and respect because they are human beings. I believe that is a concept that people can hang on to and that it's sufficiently concrete.

What human rights mean

Our findings revealed that the voluntary sector has a broad understanding of human rights principles but that these are not necessarily drawn from the Human Rights Act. Respondents to the questionnaire drew a distinction between usage of the Human Rights Act and reliance on human rights principles. Several respondents highlighted that they are not the same thing. An umbrella organisation replying to the questionnaire commented that they would use human rights in their policy work both nationally and regionally with the proviso that:

> The concept of human rights is a loose one for us and not necessarily tied down to the Human Rights Act [in fact I'm] not aware that we use the Act at all. It is possible to rely on concepts like dignity and respect and it is necessary to put the focus on individuals and their rights.

A membership organisation in Wales noted that:

> Some organisations do use the word 'rights but it's not necessarily based on the Human Rights Act. Disability and children's groups seem to be the ones who use the language of 'rights'.

The overall picture was summarised by one large organisation working in social care, which commented that their awareness of human rights was 'poor in terms of legislation, but adequate in terms of human rights as an issue.' The following responses to a question asking organisations to define what they meant by a 'rights-based' approach reveal both the breadth of the definition and the consistency of the common themes.

- 'Empowering learning disabled people to live free from abuse.'

- 'Promoting equality and fair access to services and opportunities.'

- 'We promote conceptions of universal human rights, which our particular clients require but lack.'

- 'We fight for equal rights.'

- 'We are explicitly committed to placing service-users' autonomy at the centre of mental healthcare.'

- 'We aim to empower carers to make choices and take control of their lives

- 'Inclusiveness and equalities.'

- 'Everyone has the right to a decent home that truly meets their needs.'

It is not yet widely acknowledged that the Human Rights Act's purpose is to assist in achieving these goals and that the Convention rights are relevant to rights-based approaches. Yet voluntary organisations are founded on the values underpinning the Universal Declaration and the Human Rights Act and the potential for convergence is waiting to be realised. A seminar participant made this link by asking:

> Is there any shared understanding of human rights? The voluntary sector work on issues based on the fundamental values in our society. They have worked these values out so they could lead the debate.

Until organisations recognise this connection and devise an institutional strategy that embraces it, the Act is likely to remain under-used for social justice purposes.

A proposed framework

How could organisations, large and small, devise a human rights strategy? By amalgamating specific and general conceptions, a meaning of 'human rights' may be reached that is accessible and workable in practice. Each organisation should reflect on what is most appropriate for its own strategic goals but we suggest the following as a possible framework.

Given the unacceptable but persistent fact that socially excluded and vulnerable people continue to experience poor services, ill-treatment and discrimination, those working on their behalf should adopt an approach that recognises that these may constitute failures to protect the human rights of those individuals. The basis for the improvement of these conditions should be the requirements on policy-makers and service providers to respect human rights and to be accountable for them. The human rights involved include, at minimum:

Respect and dignity

- Recognition that all individuals have human rights which derive from their humanity

- Respect for the person, the home and the family

- Right to be free from degrading treatment

Equality

- Non-discrimination against particular groups

- Social inclusion

Rights that may be relevant in particular circumstances

- Right to life

- Right to liberty

- Right to private and family life

- Freedom of thought, conscience and religion

- Freedom of expression

- Freedom of association

- Right to marry and found a family

- Right to education

- Right to enjoyment of property

Fair hearing rights
- Fair procedures

- Participation

- Autonomy

This list does not attempt to be definitive but to represent a starting point for debate about designing an institutional strategy. Where expertise is available, the provisions of the international human rights instruments can be added to the framework. Two limiting factors about human rights should also be remembered. The first is that some human rights may be restricted on specified grounds (see appendix). The second is that there needs to be awareness of when requirements to comply with human rights may be legally enforced and when they are being argued for on the basis of best practice. In the latter case the requirements may be subject to audit and inspection regimes.

A role for the Commission on Equality and Human Rights

Giving specificity and coherence to the meaning and usefulness of human rights will be an important part of the new Commission's remit and it should progress this work in partnership with the voluntary and community sector. The Joint Committee on Human Rights in its report on the structure, functions and powers of the Commission recommended the following:

> We believe that the commission, in partnership with the voluntary sector, should concentrate on building up knowledge and awareness about human rights among voluntary groups so that they can use these principles in negotiations with public authorities on behalf of their constituents and in their policy and campaigning work. We see this as an essential part of the systemic work needed to develop a culture of respect for human rights and as complementary to advising individuals on their human rights and how to assert them (JCHR, 2004).

One seminar participant felt that the initiative should come from the Commission:

> The CEHR can't expect the voluntary sector to ask for help with human rights since they don't know what they are. The Commission will need to make human rights as concrete and easy as possible.

The 'common understanding' of human rights that the Universal Declaration aspires to has not yet been reached either in the voluntary sector or wider society but another seminar participant had advice for the Commission on the approach that it should take:

> The Commission will need to get the dignity and respect message right and then it will have an organising principle on how to promote human rights.

The Commission will also have to consider how practical information about the Human Rights Act can best be provided to voluntary and comunity organisations. The training methods used by the British Institute of Humn Rights in their community outreach programme could provide a useful model for human rights education. They start with practical scenarios that recipient organisations will typically be dealing with and then add the human rights dimension. Through the use of case studies they encourage participants to familiarise themselves with the different types of the Convention rights and the circumstances in which 'qualified' rights may be restricted.

Section 2

Using human rights in the voluntary
sector

5 Voluntary sector and human rights accountability

The purpose of this publication is to explore how the voluntary sector uses or could more effectively use the Human Rights Act and human rights principles to protect vulnerable and socially excluded people. This chapter explains what is included in the term 'voluntary sector' when used in this report and the different functions that voluntary and community organisations undertake. It considers in particular the sector's representative and influencing role in advancing the interests of users. The chapter goes on to outline mechanisms other than legal action available to assist voluntary organisations in holding government and other public authorities accountable for their responsibilities under the Human Rights Act. These mechanisms are developed in more detail in succeeding chapters.

The meaning of 'voluntary sector'

In this publication, the term 'voluntary sector' is used to mean organisations that exist to further the rights, interests and needs of people who are socially excluded, disadvantaged, marginalised, discriminated against and vulnerable. The introduction listed the fields in which voluntary organisations participating in the project operate. These organisations are non-governmental, non-statutory and are not managed for profit. They may or may not have charitable status.

It is, however, recognised that the term 'voluntary sector' covers a range of heterogeneous organisations and that they will not be operating in the same way or using the same approach. A distinction is drawn between the voluntary sector function of providing public services to users (which would otherwise be provided by the statutory sector) and the function of representing the interests of users of services provided by others. It is also acknowledged that many voluntary and community organisations do not provide the former types of service and that the larger ones tend to do both. Big NGOs with policy and legal departments also have the resources and expertise to use human rights principles in negotiating with government departments for changes in law or policy. Small grass-roots organisations operate under entirely different constraints.

Voluntary organisations as representatives and influencers

Voluntary organisations assist and represent people in a number of different ways. Large charities may provide information leaflets to their constituents and manage help-lines offering advice to callers. Those with a regional presence may engage in development work with regional authorities seeking to bring systemic changes to local practices. Advice and other voluntary agencies provide advice and representation in relation to a wide range of social welfare issues often dealt with in tribunals. Large and specialist NGOs may also have legal departments that can bring cases to test laws affecting their client group.

Well-resourced voluntary organisations along with specialist campaigning organisations typically have policy departments which, through research, analysis and published reports, will seek to influence government policy and (subject to charity law where applicable) press for changes in the law. They also engage with Parliament by providing briefings on bills and submitting evidence to select committees. Senior executives of these organisations frequently appear on news and current affairs programmes and provide leadership for public campaigns. Several voluntary organisations have formed coalitions and alliances that coalesce around specific policy objectives. These coalitions may be separately staffed and by focusing on discrete issues and operating flexibly, they can be highly effective. The Children's Rights Alliance for England, for example, has been campaigning for greater implementation of the UN children's rights convention, a children's rights commissioner and for abolition of the 'reasonable chastisement' defence.

These kinds of organisations are a world away from small voluntary and community organisations with one or two staff members and otherwise reliant on volunteers. Although they share the same philanthropic goals, their operational capacity is restricted and localised. They tend to concentrate on providing non-legal advice to individuals and advocacy support by negotiating with service providers, such as social services and housing associations, over specific situations on behalf of the people that they represent.

There is no doubt that the voluntary and community sector, through its work at the national, regional and local level, makes a substantial contribution to driving change in public services and pursuing the achievement of social justice. The question is whether and how the sector can utilise the Human Rights Act to help realise these objectives.

Accountability for human rights protection

Some of the scenarios affecting people's human rights referred to in chapter 1 have been tested in court; others have not been but arguably they should not have to be. They all engage Convention rights and it should be possible for many of these situations to be remedied without recourse to law. Social justice is not only achievable through legal justice and the meaning of the term 'access to justice' should not be restricted to 'access to the courts.' It should mean redress for the individual concerned for the wrong committed and changes being made to policy and practice to prevent such wrongs from happening again. The Act provides a remedy in the courts for 'victims' of unlawful acts. For individuals to be able to argue for human rights compliance without having to characterise themselves as 'victims' is both desirable and empowering.

Our purpose is not to criticise the function of litigation or underplay its significance but to suggest complementary strategies that can be adopted for differing circumstances. The proposals made in this report should not be regarded as substitutes for improving advice and representation services or increasing legal aid provision. We do, however, address the ways in which the voluntary sector uses legal action in chapter 7 because of its significance as a means of accountability and because it is a strategy that voluntary organisations can pursue.

The purpose instead is to look at ways in which voluntary organisations can use the Human Rights Act to influence improvements in public services, particularly in their capacity as advocates for service users (which may include representation in legal proceedings in which users are involved). The assumption is that voluntary organisations can seek to hold public authorities accountable for their legal responsibilities by using preventative mechanisms in addition to or in place of initiating legal action. Because of the lack of acknowledgment by the Government and elsewhere of such a function, this has been an expedition into relatively uncharted territory.

What are the mechanisms that can be used for enforcing human rights compliance outside the courts? Other options for holding public authorities accountable are not provided for in the legislation. They are, however, available and can be relied on by voluntary organisations.

The doctrine of positive obligations has already been described and it is an important factor to consider in enforcing Convention rights outside the courts. Public authorities may, in certain circumstances, be required to do more than the minimum to avoid a breach of someone's human rights. The voluntary sector can seek to negotiate for better conditions for service users by emphasising that a positive approach is required by law. Emphasising the benefits of positive compliance is often more productive in reaching a resolution of the problem than alleging a breach of the law which is more likely to have adversarial consequences. Public authorities themselves see the virtue in preventative strategies and (naturally as potential respondents) prefer to avoid the risk of costly litigation.

It is often unclear, however, whether failures to revise procedures or practices will in fact constitute a breach of the law. Voluntary organisations will be reluctant to suggest that this is the case without being confident that such a claim is reasonably justifiable. Another useful factor that can be brought into play, therefore in the grey area between clear legal breach and obvious bad practice is the inspection regime on human rights being developed by the Audit Commission and other inspectorates. Public authorities are increasingly being required to demonstrate that they have implemented human rights considerations into their policies and practices for inspection purposes. Inspections therefore constitute a mechanism for holding public authorities accountable for human rights protection and voluntary organisations can engage proactively with the inspection process. Positive obligations and the role of the inspectorates are explored further in the chapter on improving procedure and practice.

The Commission for Equality and Human Rights will be a public institution charged with the promotion and protection of human rights. Because it will not be able to support individuals in bringing legal proceedings under the Human Rights Act, it will be seeking alternative strategies for ensuring protection of Convention rights. The Commission will, for example, be empowered to conduct inquiries into suspected breaches of Convention rights and make recommendations for action, which should drive changes in policy and practice. The voluntary sector will play an essential part in bringing information about alleged violations to the Commission's attention so that inquiries can be initiated.

Government should be held accountable for its own exhortations. The Lord Chancellor forecast that public institutions would be 'habitually, automatically responsive to human rights considerations' (Irvine, 2001). The institutional transformation towards a culture of respect for human rights is not only required of regional and local public authorities but of government as well. But who will remind government of its rhetoric and its responsibility? What is missing at the moment is a complementary and parallel strategy within the voluntary sector to develop and use methods for holding public authorities accountable for their human rights responsibilities on behalf of service users. Policy work with government and parliament and advocacy and development work with public authorities in the regions provide opportunities to introduce human rights points to strengthen the arguments being made. By making progress in such areas, voluntary organisations can share experiences and thereby influence other voluntary organisations.

In succeeding chapters we consider the practicalities of using human rights in these contexts and test the assumption about accountability. The fact that promotion of human rights is now a recognised charitable objective assists charities that have previously felt constrained from pursuing human rights arguments for fear of attracting criticism from the Charity Commission. It may also enable other organisations that have explicitly focused on human rights issues to become charities (Charity Commission, 2003).

We go on to record experiences of implementing rights-based approaches in general before considering how a human rights approach could be used in specific circumstances.

A human rights approach: general points

Many organisations working across the voluntary sector have an understanding of the potential for human rights principles to empower disadvantaged groups and help them achieve the changes that are needed. Two-thirds of organisations responding to the questionnaire said in relation to 'achieving the goals' of their organisation that 'human rights are perceived to be' either 'very useful' or 'quite useful.' Two-thirds also said that they frequently or sometimes use a 'rights-based' approach in their work.

Some organisations, however, do not use human rights or a rights-based approach. Seven out thirty organisations replying to the questionnaire felt that human rights are of 'limited usefulness' and one medium-size organisation describing itself as providing 'support to the voluntary sector' replied that human rights are 'not useful at all.' We have not considered the advantages of a rights-based strategy in contrast to other strategies for advancing the interests of people represented by the voluntary sector. Some organisations, for example, find that to highlight inefficiencies in services may be more productive in getting immediate results. For some people working directly with service users there was a concern that human rights seem to involve an assertion of individual rights, which may be inappropriate in certain circumstances. As a participant at the Newcastle seminar put it:

> The attitude among some people particularly the elderly seems to be: what are we complaining about when we've got more than we had or, for refugees, what we have left behind.

One person working with people with learning difficulties told us:

> There has been a cultural change in learning disability but we have found that it can be counter-productive to assert rights.

Although a fifth of respondents to the questionnaire agreed that the Human Rights Act 'seems relevant, but doesn't meet with a good response; it might be counter-productive,' three-fifths disagreed with this proposition (the majority disagreeing 'strongly'). Another fifth said that they did not know.

A clear majority among voluntary organisations consulted during our project preferred, as a matter of principle, to characterise the interests of the people that they are representing in terms of rights rather than needs because of the potential this allows for empowerment and greater autonomy for the individuals concerned. One seminar participant drew a distinction between different kinds of rights:

> Disabled groups have tended to use 'civil rights' rather than 'human rights'. But human rights are more fundamental and the government can't take them away.

Some voluntary organisations, however, report difficulties in using human rights in practice and with effect, outside a litigation context. One respondent to the survey from a large NGO commented that the 'aim framework' of rights-based approaches was generally understood but 'the implementation less so.' As he described it, the approach has to be grounded in practical suggestions rather than theoretical claims:

> We have struggled to give greater definition to a rights-based approach. People in poverty feel that they're not respected or treated with dignity but there's conditionality about using rights-based language. Something practical like arguing for more participation will make the case more attractive. We find that this is more effective than a philosophical claim of rights.

Someone from another large charity described the approach as a pragmatic one:

> We use the language of rights where it will be well-received and where it is acceptable in discourse. For example, the NHS doesn't use human rights language at all.

Some people at the seminars mentioned the difficulties that voluntary organisations might have in using human rights arguments to challenge other organisations that may be providing their funds. Because the voluntary sector is mainly funded from public or statutory sources and usually for specific projects, the feeling was that:

> The funders are not interested in seeing them do human rights work and they can't just add it in.

The observation that funders will not support 'human rights' projects suggests that more work needs to be done to educate funders on the connection between human rights principles and the social justice programmes that they are committed to supporting.

The fact that every person has human rights is a complicating factor when rights conflict. More guidance on using a human rights framework to accommodate competing rights is needed. A seminar participant noted:

> It's a challenge for voluntary organisations to use the voices of the people whom they represent. It's particularly difficult to use a rights-based approach because the rights of so many people are involved, like children, parents, teachers etc.

A provider of healthcare services gave the following analysis of the different approaches that the Human Rights Act offers:

> The discussion about human rights is taking place on two levels. Firstly, there is the Human Rights Act as a weapon. An example of that is in relation to detentions of terrorist suspects in Belmarsh where it's a valuable weapon.
>
> But in other areas, weapons can be a disadvantage, for example, in healthcare they lead to a more defensive attitude. In those cases, it

would be better to use human rights as a 'design tool' by giving positive emphasis to compliance. The message needs to be not that you're relying on negativistic laws but proposing that individuals should be put at the centre of decision-making. The approach should be that you're doing something right if you respect people's rights rather than if you are being forced to.

The representative of a large NGO acknowledged that although there was institutional commitment to a rights-based approach, there was inconsistency within the organisation. There is reluctance, for example, within press and fund-raising departments to emphasise 'rights' but she recognised that 'we should practise what we preach.'

Save the Children UK is another large organisation working to resolve discrepancies of approach internally. As an internal briefing paper describes it, rights-based approaches have long been incorporated from the 'bottom-up' in development programmes but now the charity is adopting a 'systematic shift' to a rights-based approach across the organisation. The approach is being built into 'higher-level decision-making' and is regarded as 'non-negotiable.' Save the Children's aim is to:

> seek to persuade people that a rights-based approach is more respectful of children, and that it maximises sustainability, efficiency and overall impact.

Some organisations, however, had reportedly done things the other way round. They had trained senior staff on the implications of the Act but not front-line staff who are working with service users in the field. People wanted guidance on how human rights can be used in practice in every day situations. One seminar participant identified emerging trends and how lessons can be learned from other sectors:

> Can the low expectations of service users be tackled via the Human Rights Act? We're witnessing a shift in attitude from needs to claims, from charity to justice. Compare the progress on this made by disability groups, which have a unified and powerful political consciousness with a dignified understanding of rights.

The overwhelming message from seminar discussions was that voluntary organisations were keen to explore ways in which human rights principles could be used more effectively and to share experiences with other organisations. One person now employed at an age charity who had previously worked for a disability organisation commented that in terms of using rights-based approaches, 'age is fifteen years behind disability.' Coalitions and alliances were seen to be particularly useful because they tend to focus on specific objectives and use a rights-based approach. The following chapters consider specific areas where the voluntary sector is using or could use human rights principles.

6 Implementing a human rights approach

The rest of this report looks at ways that voluntary organisations can use a human rights framework in their work. It is evident that they will need considerable information and support both to absorb human rights into their strategies and then to implement them. Where should voluntary organisations best direct the energy and resources required? Available evidence suggests that the voluntary sector should prioritise using human rights principles with public authorities where legal responsibilities reside.

Working with individuals and client groups

Voluntary sector organisations regularly give information and advice to users of services. The intention is that individuals, once equipped with the information, can use it in their own negotiations with the providers of services. It is not possible in terms of resources for the voluntary sector to take on responsibility for pursuing the many complaints that are brought to their attention by individuals. The purpose of giving help and advice is to empower and support the complainant in seeking a resolution to their complaint themselves. There are, however, many individuals who find it difficult to make complaints and assert their rights and they remain excluded from remedies to which they are entitled unless someone pursues the matter on their behalf. Research has shown that one in five people takes no action to solve their problem (whatever it is) and around one million problems go unsolved each year because people do not understand their basic rights or know how to seek help (Pleasence, 2004).

Many of the large voluntary organisations offer helpline services and publish information leaflets designed for users telling them 'what your rights are'. These are not necessarily rights as specified in human rights law but rather under an applicable statute such as rights to housing and benefits. Levels of awareness of human rights among the clients of the thirty organisations responding to the questionnaire and within the sector in general, were overwhelming believed to be 'patchy' or 'poor'.

Awareness about rights to services is often lacking too. This is particularly the case in the age sector. Although the organisations working to help older people consulted during this project are explicitly using a rights-based approach, they report a culture of reluctance among older people to 'claim' their rights. The generation that experienced the hardships of the Second World War is more accustomed to thinking about duties than rights. The

Something for Everyone report found that organisations working with older people 'mentioned a generational difference in attitude by older people towards the whole concept of rights' and that older people 'don't know what their basic rights are in terms of the services that they receive' let alone about the Human Rights Act (BIHR, 2002). The head of policy at a well-known age charity has observed:

> Older people don't know that they have any rights and they don't know they have them because they are treated as if they didn't have any. There are all sorts of reasons why complaining, or challenging professionals, is extremely difficult when you are ill, disabled, feel powerless, scared, have no access to independent advice and so on.

There are clearly considerable hurdles. First, people have to find out that they have rights in an environment that is resistant to this knowledge being available. But even if there is consciousness about the existence of rights there is great difficulty in accessing them effectively. If people are so unaware of their legal entitlements to public services, how can their right to protection under the Human Rights Act be brought to their attention in ways that they can use? The consensus among voluntary organisations working in the age sector was that trying to use human rights principles to empower older people would be unsuccessful. Vague and aspirant principles will not help people who already find it difficult to access specific entitlements. It was considered to be more productive at present to use human rights discourse with the relevant professionals.

Levels of confidence and articulacy among individuals experiencing disadvantage and discrimination vary and the examples given from the age sector cannot be extrapolated more generally. Each voluntary organisation will adopt its own approach in seeking to empower the people whose interests it is promoting. This report concentrates, however, on ways in which voluntary organisations can use human rights with public authorities because that is where legal responsibility lies and where there is potential for tangible results. The following example, provided by a seminar participant who works as an advocate, illustrates what can happen when the burden is placed on individuals to assert their rights rather than the professionals to safeguard them:

> Institutions can impose limitations and restrictions that fundamentally affect people's freedoms and their rights. We speak to people about what they can do in these situations but we find they can be persuaded out of their complaints – in fact they are bullied. It may be worse if they refer to their human rights – it could create more antagonism.

Clearly there may be risks for vulnerable service users in claiming their rights. This makes work on institutional change more imperative.

Working with public authorities

The proposition is that if the voluntary sector can introduce human rights concepts into their work with public authorities this should contribute to greater understanding within public authorities of their legal responsibilities under the Human Rights Act. The consequence should be improved compliance and therefore better protection of individuals' human rights. There is also likely to be less litigation. This approach provides an opportunity for the voluntary sector because it will complement initiatives on human rights compliance currently being undertaken within the public sector. We refer to these first because they provide the context for what the voluntary sector can do.

What does the law require?

As referred to above, public authorities have legal responsibilities under Human Rights Act to act compatibly with Convention rights. Under the doctrine of 'positive obligations', the legal requirement is not limited to avoiding the breach of human rights but extends to adopting a positive approach to protecting human rights. In practical terms, the former tends to involve risk assessments and monitoring of legal cases by the legal department whereas the latter involves a cultural change throughout the whole organisation, particularly among staff delivering services to the public. The Government's guidance booklet distributed to public authorities before the Act came into force explained the requirements as follows:

> All public authorities have a positive obligation to ensure that respect for human rights is at the core of their day-to-day work. This means that you should act in a way that positively reinforces the principles of the Human Rights Act...you have a crucial human rights role to play, not only in ensuring that you always act in accordance with the Convention rights, but also in supporting a positive attitude to human rights issues throughout the community. This is a vital responsibility for all of us (Home Office, 2000).

Evidence has shown that the 'positive obligations' message has failed to take root within most public authorities (JCHR, 6th report, 2003). The results of recent research conducted by the Audit Commission among 175 public bodies were that 58% had no strategy 'or clear corporate approach' for human rights and that 'in many local authorities the Act has not left the desk of the lawyers.' 73% of health trusts were reportedly 'not taking any action' (Audit Commission, 2003).

These findings are likely to be due to at least three reasons. Firstly, the 'positive obligations' requirement derives from cases decided by the Strasbourg court (and increasingly the UK courts), rather than the face of the statute. Therefore the principle is not widely known or understood by people coming to the subject for the first time. Secondly, the practical implications of 'supporting a positive attitude' are not clear and cannot easily be translated across the several departments providing public services. Thirdly, because the concept involves nebulous things like the way of approaching a problem rather than a right or wrong answer, the legal department is not best suited to be responsible for implementation. Embedding a human rights culture within a public authority calls for a different kind of education process (more like change management) and requires leadership from senior executives and political leaders. It also requires that human rights principles explicitly inform the development of policies and practices.

In reporting on its inquiry into the case for a human rights commission, the Joint Committee on Human Rights found that:

> Too often human rights are looked upon as something from which the state needs to defend itself, rather than to promote as its core ethical values. There is a failure to recognise the part that they could play in promoting social justice and social inclusion and in the drive to improve public services. We have found widespread evidence of a lack of respect for the rights of those who use public services, especially the rights of those who are most vulnerable and in need of protection (JCHR, 6th report, 2003).

What does it mean in practice?

The principal message that public authorities need to receive is that compliance with the Human Rights Act complements what they should already be doing. It should connect with equality and diversity policies, ethical governance standards and it should be regarded as central to improving public services. The Audit Commission has taken a proactive and visible lead by emphasising these links. As it explained in its report published in 2003:

> The Human Rights Act can help to improve public services, as it seeks to ensure the delivery of quality services that meet the needs of individual service users (Audit Commission, 2003).

The guidance provided by the Audit Commission and others suggests that public authorities should:

- use human rights principles to inform decision-making (e.g. does the action taken protect a person's right to private and family life);

- avoid blanket policies and procedures because these fail to put the individual at the centre of the decision;

- balance competing rights because human rights are as much for the many as for the few (e.g., in the case of noisy neighbours and school exclusions; the case of the white hospital patient who refused to be treated by black medical staff); and

- make the connection between human rights, equalities and service improvements (practices and procedures should be reviewed collectively rather than separately for different pieces of legislation).

The Audit Commission is progressing its work in this area and is due to consult shortly on including human rights in its 'key lines of enquiry' in Comprehensive Performance Assessments requirements for local authorities. The statutory inspection process is likely to be the most significant mechanism for evaluating compliance with the 'positive obligations' under the Human Rights Act. It also requires action to be taken on the basis of best practice in addition to the minimum required to avoid legal challenge. These sorts of considerations will shape the decisions and priorities of public bodies.

Notwithstanding the considerable work put in by the Audit Commission and others, many public authorities have difficulty in understanding the practical implications of what they are required to do. The legal officer at a northern council reported that the service delivery departments were forwarding the Audit Commission guidance that they were receiving on to the legal department with notes asking 'what do we have to do?' A seminar participant gave an example of this difficulty:

> For doctors, the idea that people have positive rights needs thinking about. For example, if I have a long waiting list and the effect is that someone is excluded from access to me, is that an abuse of that person's human rights?

The answer is that long waiting lists or denial of access to a particular doctor are not themselves a breach of human rights but the consequences might be. Healthcare providers must think of patients as holders of human rights as much as they have been trained to think of them as 'customers'. Therefore medical professionals need to take care to consider the effects of these practical problems on individual patients in human rights terms. In this scenario, the need to treat patients with respect and dignity, consider their right to private and family life and perhaps even their right to life will have to be taken into account in the difficult business of juggling waiting lists.

What will it cost?

As that example shows, the principal cost of a positive approach towards human rights implementation will be the education of staff responsible for delivering services. The training programmes should integrate human rights, equalities and ethical standards. To be effective, adherence to human rights standards should be built into employee appraisals. The way in which front-line staff members treat service users (with rather than without respect) should not itself attract financial cost. It is notable that the Audit Commission report refers to the cost of litigation rather than the cost of compliance by public authorities. The emphasis is on what can be saved by pursuing a preventative approach.

A public sector duty to promote human rights?

Another issue that is relevant to public sector compliance and therefore to voluntary sector engagement is law reform. Although this question is outside the current remit because research has not been undertaken into its impact on the public sector, we raised it with seminar participants to see what their reactions were. Some findings on it are included in this report because of the likelihood that a clear legal duty (rather than a collection of principles from court cases) would provide something concrete for the voluntary sector to base a human rights argument on when negotiating with public authorities.

As has been mentioned, public sector duties to promote equality in addition to existing measures to tackle discrimination have been legislated for in relation to race and are promised for disability and gender. They also apply in Northern Ireland, the Welsh Assembly and the Greater London Authority. The chair of the Equal Opportunities Commission recently gave her view of the rationale for them:

> Nearly 30 years of enforcing sex discrimination legislation has convinced us that we need to lift the burden of taking action off individuals and onto institutions.

The Joint Committee on Human Rights has concluded that a positive duty is needed for human rights:

> the statutory requirement to act compatibly with human rights is not enough on its own....we are now persuaded by the evidence that imposing a 'positive' or 'general' duty on public authorities to promote human rights will be an effective way of advancing [the need for greater focus by public authorities on their positive obligations to protect human rights] (JCHR, 11th report, 2004).

Most organisations responding to the questionnaire agreed that a positive duty 'might be useful in helping the voluntary sector use the Human Rights Act or human rights concepts more effectively.' Opinions among seminar participants on the positive duty question included the following observations from those in favour:

- public authorities aren't getting the 'positive obligations' message at all;

- without a positive duty, public authorities won't do anything;

- you can't leave it to individuals to assert their rights, you have to get organisations to change; and

- if I were a public authority I'd welcome a single message on diversity and human rights.

Others felt that an opportunity should be given to the Commission on Equality and Human Rights to see if it could 'bring out the positive obligations concept more with public authorities.' Since the Government has not responded favourably to the JCHR's recommendation, it is likely that the matter will be left to the new Commission to investigate. The effects on public authorities and the potential benefits for individuals and society of a positive duty to promote human rights or even a single and combined duty to promote equality and human rights deserve consideration.

In the meantime, it is clear that administrative competence and confidence on human rights need to be developed within all public authorities developing policies and providing services. Public authorities need to be encouraged to absorb human rights thinking within an environment of competing demands on time and resources. Although they are subject to active encouragement by the Audit Commission (and increasingly the other inspectorates), there is little being done by the voluntary and community sector to reinforce these messages.

The promotion by public authorities of a culture of respect for human rights, equality and diversity would be likely to improve the delivery of public services and so benefit the disadvantaged and vulnerable people using them. This will not happen within public authorities overnight and pressure for action needs to come from the voluntary and community sector. The next two chapters consider practical ways in which voluntary organisations use or could use human rights firstly in influencing national policy and secondly in changing procedure and practice at the local level.

7 Influencing policy

This chapter examines the ways in which voluntary organisations can seek to hold government accountable for its human rights obligations. Policy work is an important function of large and specialist voluntary organisations and many have also formed coalitions, which then concentrate on seeking particular changes in law and policy. The work involves research, publication of reports and meetings with Whitehall officials and with ministers. Voluntary organisations also provide briefings on bills to members of Parliament and evidence to select committees. This report is predominately concerned with using the Human Rights Act outside a litigation context but reference is made to test cases because of their significance in driving social change. The use of human rights in public campaigns and by the media is also considered.

Working with government

The government is a public authority for the purposes of the Human Rights Act and it also has treaty obligations to implement international human rights instruments. The requirement to comply with human rights extends beyond the development of legislation and policy in Whitehall to supporting regional public authorities for which government departments are responsible. Voluntary organisations report using human rights principles with government to support the policy positions being advanced. A large charity working with disabled adults told us:

> The Human Rights Act is seen as another tool to fit with what's already available. We have found that there has been a greater role for the Act in political campaigning (both with government and parliament) rather than in individual negotiation.

Another campaigner on race equality commented:

> We have had some success with using the UN human rights mechanisms to challenge government thinking. The language of human rights has offered an opportunity to race groups, which were focusing on particular discrimination issues, to show that their arguments were universal. It meant that the message could be that challenging racism wasn't about looking for special privileges.

But the Human Rights Act is often still regarded within Whitehall primarily as a legal matter. A representative from a large NGO told one seminar:

If you talk to civil servants about rights, you feel the shutters going down. Their response is: shouldn't the courts be deciding that? We find it hard to make progress with rights. What are the routes that we can use?

Some people reported disillusionment because the Government is itself not seen to be respecting human rights. The prevailing emphasis within Government on responsibilities over rights also inhibits discourse based on the human rights of the most impoverished people in society. Yet, as has been observed:

Poverty can undermine people's capacity to fulfil their responsibilities...[because]...the ability to contribute to or participate in society as a full citizen requires a basic level of access to essential goods, services and facilities (Lister, 2004).

A large non-governmental organisation working on social policy issues reported:

We have met considerable barriers to using a rights-based approach. We would never refer to the right to be free from poverty. Poverty in the UK is not seen to be an abuse of human rights but about lazy people scrounging benefits. Civil servants have said to us 'we can't deal with dignity and respect; you can't come and talk to us about that'.

This reported observation reveals the depth of inconsistency within government. Firstly, on the attitude to poverty in the UK, when one contrasts this comment with DFID's acknowledgment, quoted above, that poverty in other countries constitutes 'vulnerability and 'weak' voice'. Secondly, the Government is inconsistent about promoting the underlying values of human rights. Civil servants may resist talk of 'dignity and respect' but this is contrary to the message being delivered from the heart of Government. In the foreword to the White Paper on establishing the Commission for Equality and Human Rights, the Prime Minister, Tony Blair said:

We cannot achieve our vision of high quality public services for all if those services do not respect individuals' rights to dignity, privacy and respect (DTI, 2004).

The disparity of approach suggests that much work needs to be done across Whitehall to disseminate government policy on human rights but also to give specificity to concepts like 'dignity and respect'. It also suggests an unjustifiable tendency within government to differentiate between what regional and local public services are supposed to be doing and the responsibilities to which government itself is subject. The Department for Constitutional Affairs has initiated a strategic review within Whitehall of arrangements for implementing the Human Rights Act. This follows the criticisms made by the Joint Committee on Human Rights in its report on the case for a human rights commission (JCHR, 6th report, 2003). The review should improve understanding of what implementation entails and aim for consistency across government. Unfortunately the review on the Act is not connected to the separate and more formalistic review that has been recently completed of the UK's position under the international human rights instruments. The thinking at Whitehall needs to be more joined-up.

The reality is that the voluntary sector needs to be pragmatic. A seminar participant working with children and young people commented:

> Groups are reluctant to use a rights-based approach with government when it doesn't work. For example, there's a perception that the Home Office isn't interested in human rights and so if you talk to officials about the rights of children in custody you have use the language of welfare and needs otherwise the discussion gets shut down.

Is it effective to use human rights language with government? As another seminar participant put it drily, 'if it's not working then it's not a good investment'. Voluntary organisations looking to avoid counter-productive encounters with Whitehall officials will have to find more subtle approaches. Some may find that progress can be made by emphasising, not so much that individuals have human rights (that may still be unpalatable) but that public authorities, including government, have 'positive obligations' to respect human rights. Others may find this too defeatist but each will find the approach that works best for them and the interests they are seeking to advance.

When civil servants tell voluntary organisations that they 'can't come and talk about dignity and respect', it should be remembered that a former Home Secretary suggested that the Human Rights Act would provide the 'language you need to speak to win an argument.' The Government should be held accountable for its own rhetoric. The question is how successfully the voluntary sector can do this.

Working with parliament

It is a function of Parliament to hold governments to account and this provides opportunities for the voluntary sector to influence law and policy. There are two specific human rights mechanisms in the parliamentary process. First, there is the requirement in the Human Rights Act for ministers to make statements in Parliament about the compliance of bills with Convention rights and the procedure for reforming non-compliant legislation. Second, Parliament has established the Joint Committee on Human Rights, which undertakes a number of scrutiny functions relating to human rights in the UK.

Joint Committee on Human Rights

The Joint Committee on Human Rights enjoys a wide remit 'to consider matters relating to human rights in the United Kingdom' (excluding individual cases) and in the three years since it was established in 2001, the Committee has already made a significant impact on governmental policy. Several voluntary organisations have actively contributed to this process by submitting written evidence and giving oral evidence. The principal work of the Committee is to scrutinise draft legislation for compliance both with the ECHR and the Human Rights Act and also with the international human rights treaties to which the UK is a party. This process operates as a review of the government's own opinion about human rights compliance.

The Joint Committee has also undertaken a number of inquiries. In particular, it has reviewed institutional arrangements for supporting human rights in the UK. The Committee's reports on the case for a human rights commission (which quoted extensively from evidence provided by the voluntary sector) were influential in persuading the Government to establish the Commission for Equality and Human Rights (JCHR, 2002–04). The Committee has also reviewed the work of the Northern Ireland Human Rights Commission (JCHR, 2003).

The Joint Committee is also undertaking reviews of governmental compliance with the UN covenants and with the matters identified by the UN committees as requiring attention. It has reported on the Children's Rights Convention (JCHR, 2003), recently on the Covenant on Economic, Social and Cultural Rights (JCHR, 2004) and has commenced an inquiry into the Government's review of its international human rights commitments. The Committee also conducts inquiries into specific matters affecting human rights in the UK, such as the meaning of public authority under the Human Rights Act (JCHR, 2004) and the ongoing inquiry into deaths in custody.

Other parliamentary processes

A test of whether human rights standards are absorbed in parliamentary work is to consider their impact outside the specific human rights mechanisms. Here the voluntary sector can play a significant part in raising awareness about human rights in social policy areas. For example, the Commons select committee on health recently conducted an inquiry into elder abuse from the perspective of health policy towards the elderly. Elder abuse, however, also engages the rights of the elderly to privacy, dignity and freedom from cruel and degrading treatment. Tessa Harding of Help the Aged in her opening remarks to the select committee on health's inquiry into elder abuse said:

> I think there is a very important human rights dimension to the whole issue of elder abuse which I would like to draw to the Committee's attention (Health Committee, 2004).

In their report, the Committee concluded:

> there is no single definition of elder abuse which would satisfy every test. Nevertheless, we consider that the reference to the violation of an individual's human and civil rights...provides a useful foundation (Health Committee, 2004).

Voluntary sector briefings on draft legislation also provide an opportunity to introduce human rights points to strengthen an argument. An example comes from the field of maternity care. The Health and Social Care (Community Health and Standards) Bill proposed the expansion of welfare food (then restricted to milk) to low income pregnant women, mothers and children under a 'Healthy Start' scheme but it was subject to certain requirements being met by the beneficiaries. The conditionality aspect was subsequently removed but when the bill was at the House of Lords Report Stage, the Royal College of Nursing and the Maternity Alliance issued a joint briefing. They gave four principal reasons for their opposition to imposing conditions. These were listed as: philosophical (the principle of conditionality in respect of a welfare benefit which provides food to families in need is morally wrong); human rights (see below); practical (no evidence that financial coercion will increase service uptake); and nurse-client relationship (the health professional might be perceived as 'policing' poorer families). In relation to the human rights concern, they said-

> Human rights: The wide-ranging powers to impose requirements on beneficiaries as proposed by this Bill, and specifically the power to require a woman to submit herself or her child to medical examination and to allow health professionals or other persons into her home, may contravene the Human Rights Act, in particular Article 8 (the right to respect for private and family life).

Test case litigation

Test case litigation can be an effective mechanism for holding government and other public authorities accountable. We refer to this species of legal action here because it is one strategy that can be pursued by the voluntary sector and therefore deserves inclusion when considering the uses of human rights and because the Human Rights Act is often perceived to be mainly about legal remedies and it is worth noting how effectively they can be achieved.

Litigation, when successful, can represent the only way (apart from new legislation) to ensure that unlawful action is stopped and necessary changes put in place. Given the inequality between state agencies and the individual, the courts can operate as the sole guardians of the rights of vulnerable people. A participant in a seminar who is head of policy at a large charity expressed its importance as follows:

Improving public service and practice is key, but the shock of direct challenge is necessary to address some accepted norms of service delivery. We can become so accustomed to degrading practices, that we don't see them for what they are, which is infringements of human rights. The point about the Human Rights Act is that it enables these hidden abuses to be revealed.

Court decisions can have far-reaching implications for law, policy and practice and these can benefit large numbers of people. The principles from one case can be applied to other seemingly unrelated situations and it is often the case that the threat of legal proceedings can achieve the necessary change without the need to enter the courtroom.

Litigation has a particular role to play in explaining the meaning of and testing the limits of new legislation. It is often necessary for this process to be gone through before the law can have practical application. Convention rights particularly merit greater clarity of definition and this can only be done through judicial determination. One of our seminar participants involved in race equality work explained:

> There are benefits in litigation – it focuses the mind. When new legislation is passed, litigation is a start because it clarifies the law, so we shouldn't be surprised or too concerned that since the Human Rights Act came into force it has been dominated by litigation. Compare it with the Race Relations Act of 1976 that brought in the right to sue for racial discrimination. We had to wait till 2000 for the positive duty to promote race equality in the Race Relations (Amendment) Act.

Some organisations have a strategy to use litigation to achieve their objectives and adopt a proactive rather than reactive approach. Child Poverty Action Group have pursued a test-case approach for 25 years and use the Human Rights Act as an additional legal tool though they are often restricted by the lack of legal aid. Organisations like Stonewall and Press for Change have also used litigation because short of legislative reform, there are no other ways of achieving equality for gay and transgendered people. Other organisations with limited options available, for example those working on behalf of people with mental health problems, the travelling community and refugees, also resort to litigation:

> Human rights are really important for refugees and asylum seekers. It's the only thing they can use. They've been stripped of services like healthcare. They are not allowed to be classified as 'homeless'. Destitution followed and the only way to challenge that was to use the Human Rights Act in court.

Some organisations reported being prepared to use the Human Rights Act in a test case but have not found one. A large organisation working in the social care field reported that:

> We see the Human Rights Act as a 'tool at our disposal' but there's a problem in finding test cases.

A representative of the Muslim community identified the following problems:

> There are a number of groups on the receiving end of human rights abuses who feel that the Human Rights Act does not provide them with protection. This is true of the Muslim community. The right to religion is very vague. Are these human rights principles sufficient or does more work need to be done to clarify them? For the Muslim community though, it is difficult to pursue strategic cases because we can't make links with established organisations which have the resources to take them on.

Some voluntary organisations report more success with applications to intervene in cases that are already proceeding through the courts. For example, Victim Support intervened in a case concerning the disclosure of the previous sexual history of a victim where the court ordered that the disclosure should not be made (*R v. A* case). The Commission on Equality and Human Rights will also have the power to intervene in cases where Convention rights are at issue. It will be able to support individuals bringing cases under applicable anti-discrimination legislation and these may also involve Convention rights.

A litigation strategy using the Human Rights Act, however, can be counter-productive because it is likely to encourage a defensive response, which will not be of benefit to individuals in the long-term. Litigation may also be risky as one seminar participant explained:

> Litigating to assert rights isn't the right way forward. There are the costs involved and then there's the Government's reaction when loopholes are exposed. For example, after the Begum case on the right to enter the UK to join family members, the Government closed the door completely. The same thing happened with immigration rights for gay people (Begum and Z, A & R cases).

Test case litigation remains a specialist field. In general and for the majority of voluntary and community organisations litigation using the Human Rights Act is not feasible. As the director of a membership organisation in the North East put it:

> Litigation is not the way forward for the local voluntary sector – maybe it is for the big national charities – but for smaller organisations, there's no capacity and it's too risky.

Litigation requires participation by the individual concerned in a process, which is likely to be intimidating, confusing and stressful involving re-living the experiences complained of for a second time. This is true for many individuals who are parties to court cases but exacerbated for those who are socially excluded, inarticulate and vulnerable. It is also the case that some issues are not well-suited to litigation, not only because of the impact on the complainants themselves but also because the courts are inherently unsuited to deciding them. Closure of care homes is an example.

Public campaigns and the media

Public campaigns are often the visible face of concurrent political and policy work with government and parliament and are launched to attract popular support for the action proposed. Some voluntary organisations are specifically campaigning groups and others will pursue particular campaigns when the need arises. Some organisations proclaim themselves to be explicitly grounded in human rights. The 1990 Trust, which campaigns on behalf of black and minority ethnic communities, uses the slogan 'Human rights for race equality'. Stonewall cites Article 1 of the Universal Declaration of Human Rights, 'All human beings are born equal in dignity and rights,' prominently on its letterhead.

Some organisations said that they did not refer to human rights because of a lack of information about their relevance. The head of policy at a large well-known charity working with the most disadvantaged young people saw that their work was 'instinctively about human rights but we're not articulating it that way'. At the seminar, she made the following observations:

> We provide services and do advocacy on behalf of young people. We focus on participation by young people and their empowerment but haven't looked at human rights at all. We're also too busy fire-fighting on issues like benefits for young people to think about it. But the message that I'm picking up round the table today is, we should be using the language of human rights especially in our campaigns.

Other organisations will advertise themselves as promoting their constituents' 'rights' rather than their 'human rights'. In these cases 'rights' may be referred to without explication of the basis on which they are asserted. For example, in their recent campaign on the effects of poor housing on children, Shelter stated:

> A decent, warm, safe home should be the right of every child in this country. Over a million children do not have that right and are suffering because of it (Shelter, 2004).

A Shelter mailshot letter provides an example of the use of human rights language without attribution:

We hear about people being placed in houses with dangerous stairs, poor ventilation, defective gas fires, unsafe wiring, filthy kitchens and stinking toilets. We hear about children suffering from bronchitis, asthma and stomach aches because of their disgusting living conditions. We hear of parents sinking into depression as they struggle to cope. We can't let this go on. It's degrading, inhuman and plain wrong (Shelter, 2003).

Here, Shelter are using the wording of Article 3 which prohibits 'inhuman and degrading treatment' but do not go on to claim 'and is in breach of their human rights.' Some organisations reported concerns about referring to human rights publicly because it could be ineffective or even counterproductive. A large charity caring for disabled adults told us that although they use human rights arguments in policy work, they have not made express reference to human rights in communications with the public.

Campaigning, however, is a subtle art and there may be opportunities to present a combination of messages in a sympathetic outlet. In June 2004, the Children are Unbeatable! Alliance published a full-page advertisement in the Guardian calling for the abolition of the 'reasonable chastisement' defence. The short commentary was headed 'Equal protection from assault for our children' and asked:

In the interests of equality, human rights and child protection, please support this campaign to modernise the law on assault (*Guardian*, 21.6.04).

At a seminar the following day, we asked a children's rights campaigner about the rationale for expressing the campaign in those terms. She told us that:

The advertisement in yesterday's Guardian is an example of the need to mention all aspects: equality, human rights and child protection, in order to gain support. Because sometimes rights are seen to be conflicting with welfare, we need to use both in our public campaigning messages.

Public campaigns will often be tied to requests for donations and organisations will be sensitive to public reactions to their cause and the arguments they put forward to justify them. These reactions are assumed to be influenced by the media, certain sections of which are hostile to the application of human rights in the UK. The coordinator of a coalition of voluntary organisations told us:

Some organisations are wary of using the language of rights because of public understanding of what human rights mean based on how they're characterised by the tabloids. The Daily Mail version of human rights gets more of an airing than Francesca Klug's. There is no understanding at all among certain sections of the population that poverty exists, that gender inequality continues or that human rights abuses happen in the UK.

As already mentioned, earlier this year, the *Daily Mirror* published an extensive feature on the abuse of elderly people in the UK. The paper characterised the examples as 'a sickening catalogue of torture, abuse and neglect' but did not explicitly suggest that they constituted violations of human rights. Readers were invited to cut out a coupon sponsored by Action of Elder Abuse and it was only in the coupon that the 'rights of the elderly' were referred to.

Several seminar participants reported difficulties with perceptions of human rights, where they have come from and the poor reputation they have among journalists. There are many examples displaying the lack of information within the media about human rights in the UK. The presenter on a BBC Radio 4 current affairs programme referred to the 'European Human Rights Act' when reporting on the Conservative Party's announcement that it would review the Act. A print journalist, when asking us about this project, said:

> Didn't the Human Rights Act come into law through an EU directive? Does the Act have anything to do with charities in the UK or does it only relate to ones working internationally?

A representative of a national charity working in a regional office in the North East told us:

> There is political and popular resistance to the notion of imposing human rights standards from Europe. It conflicts with home-grown notions of liberty and freedom. We need to improve the image of human rights and get rid of 'European' in the title. The Government won't do anything till these perceptions have changed.

Another person attending the seminar who works on community projects agreed:

> The media is problematic. The Human Rights Act is seen as another imposition from Europe. We need constantly to be putting the counter case and following up in the debate.

Some organisations are recognising the obstacles and investigating how they might be overcome. A victim support group said that:

> We are looking at whether the Human Rights Act can give victims protection from media intrusion and have found that emphasising that human rights involve the balancing of rights is important. The Human Rights Act principles can be a way of easing some of the tensions. Examples are things like: victims versus defendants, service-users versus providers, family member carers versus dependant eld-

erly relatives. The media need to hear the message about the way in which rights are balanced in order for public perceptions about human rights to improve.

Other organisations have found that emphasising the universality principle underpinning human rights can contribute to greater public understanding and acceptance of minority interests. As Stonewall has observed:

> We know from our own experience that the public are much more persuaded to support the rights of lesbians and gay men if the claim for such rights is situated in the context of the more universal values of human rights and equality. The principle of equality can only have real effect in our society if it can be demonstrated that it is the right of every citizen, not a series of special measures to protect certain groups (JCHR, 22nd report, 2002).

It may be that in time the idea that human rights are 'something for everyone' will resonate with the media and with the public and that this will allow the development of a culture of respect for human rights and equality. As the reported experiences show, this is an area where the voluntary sector needs to adopt a thoughtful and sensitive strategy.

8 Improving procedure and practice

What are the ways in which the voluntary and community sector can use human rights principles to achieve improvements in procedure and practice at the local level? Since seventy percent of voluntary organisations operate locally (NCVO, 2004), this is where the greatest potential for change lies. We look both at the opportunities for introducing human rights into development and education work in partnership with the public sector as well as using human rights arguments in advocacy and representation services on behalf of individuals or groups. By public authorities in this chapter, we mean regional and local service providers such as local authorities, social services, education and housing departments, health trusts and police authorities (rather than central government which was covered in the preceding chapter). (Also included by implication are private and voluntary providers of public services as already discussed.)

Development work

Well-resourced NGOs engage in development work with public authorities, which seeks to change practice and procedure systemically in order to achieve improvements. As the trustee of a learning disability trust put the problem:

> There is a culture in which people are dismayingly grateful for inadequate services.

Save the Children operates a programme in England which seeks to influence policy makers and providers of services and explicitly introduces human rights principles (usually derived from the UN convention on the rights of the child) into the work. They tend to rely on concepts like equity, non-discrimination and participation in order to fill in gaps in provision rather than referring to specific pieces of legislation. Human rights principles are seen to be the context for the discussion rather than the basis for bald statements about the need to comply although discussions would also include reference to legal obligations where rights are clearly being infringed.

When the change that needs to be made is obvious and is easily capable of being achieved, the human rights arguments can be added to the narrative. Child Poverty Action Group has been running a campaign about access to free school meals. At the seminar in March, the human rights thinking behind it was explained:

Children experience social exclusion when their parents can't afford to buy school uniform or the children are stigmatised when free school meals are served separately. We would aim to encourage the school to make practical changes like giving children a swipe card to get their meals. We would use human rights arguments to achieve these sorts of changes which are grounded in best practice arguments rather than threats of litigation. Schools would benefit from best-practice codes on these sorts of issues.

This kind of approach reflects the success of the 'design tool' model proposed by a seminar participant and referred to earlier. Victim Support have started looking at the implications of human rights in social policy, for example, victims' rights in relation to employment and housing (Victim Support, 2003). A seminar participant with considerable experience of the voluntary sector saw the potential as follows:

Local authority and voluntary sector relations are not only about limitations on what you can do with funding for particular programmes or taking cases against local authorities. For the voluntary sector working on the ground, there is real potential for them to show the public sector, by example, how to bring human rights into their agenda. We miss a trick if we don't use the opportunities that exist for partnership working between the voluntary and public sector: this is at the coalface.

Education and training

There are opportunities within existing local partnership arrangements between the public and voluntary sectors to introduce human rights thinking. Many seminar participants recognised the value of raising awareness of human rights issues with their own staff, with users and with staff in public authorities providing services. A trustee of a learning disability trust providing local services was concerned that this was not happening because:

It is just as important as finding legal test cases in increasing confidence in the Human Rights Act to enable further empowerment. We're looking for opportunities to open this up.

One local community health organisation reported that they have prepared and distributed training packages for GPs because they could see that 'changing operational practice is key.' But the view was also that:

Of all the models of partnership working between the voluntary and public sectors, it seems that the human rights one is the most difficult.

Collaborative working between the public and voluntary sector appears to be a fruitful area for the Commission for Equality and Human Rights to explore.

The notion that public service providers can be held accountable for their responsibilities without litigation is an attractive one. The Audit Commission is already pursuing this through the audit and inspection process. The voluntary sector needs information and encouragement from a central source to be able to make their own contribution to achieving this goal.

Advocacy work

Most voluntary and community groups undertake some form of advocacy work or negotiation over the individual circumstances of their constituents. The rationale for using human rights in negotiating with service providers is to strengthen the case for change. Voluntary sector organisations, however, report difficulties in referring to human rights. Few people other than lawyers and specialists are up-to-date on legislative detail and interpretation by the courts. This lack of expertise can inhibit staff within voluntary organisations from referring to human rights when they are not familiar with the current legal position. No one wants to make an assertion that cannot be justified. Similarly, staff in public authorities who are engaged in providing services, are unlikely to be familiar with human rights principles and will tend to refer an issue to the legal department if a 'human rights point comes up.'

It should be possible, however, for staff to be sufficiently briefed on the practical application of human rights principles to any given situation in which they could arise. This is what seems to be missing for the voluntary sector (and the statutory sector too). Greater familiarity with these principles will bring greater confidence in using them. Arguably it should not be necessary to know the details of the latest case to be able to assert that principles of private or family life are at issue or that a particular practice constitutes degrading treatment. The point is not to try to win a legal argument but a principled one based on rights and values.

It is often a question of timing or of tone whether the arguments are used as a precursor to threatening legal action or in a way that seeks resolution. The manager of the BIHR community outreach programme admitted that 'it is hard to negotiate without authority on such matters, but progress can still be made.' She gave an example of how an organisation had reportedly achieved practical change through using the Human Rights Act in this way:

> A health authority had implemented a policy of prohibiting mental health in-patients from getting together in groups of more than two. The reason that was given was a concern about security but it was a blanket policy and had been imposed irrespective of whether in fact there were security problems. The voluntary organisation on behalf of an individual patient pointed this out to the health authority in a letter (claiming the right to free association) and the practice was reviewed.

Blanket policies are usually susceptible to challenge. Someone abusing drugs or alcohol may be evicted from a public library one afternoon because of a particular incident but it would not be proportionate to impose an indefinite ban on that person.

It is more problematic when the issue cannot be easily resolved and the human rights arguments have to be balanced against other considerations such as costs and resources. Even though the objective may not in the end be achieved, it may still be worth framing the discussion in terms of human rights (using the language). The purpose of raising human rights principles with service providers is to encourage them to take such principles into account in their decisions, as they are required to do by law. A good example of this is closure of care homes, which has been scrutinised in the courts on human rights grounds and the subject of guidance since. A large age charity told us:

> Article 8 is used in cases where care homes are being closed. We are highlighting that it is a human rights issue and have had a fairly positive response from care home providers.

Large organisations are more able to use these arguments because they now have a good deal of awareness of human rights issues and their application to practical situations. It is difficult for under-resourced organisations without that body of knowledge to rely on human rights arguments in a persuasive way. A small refugee support group based in the North East told us:

> We do use the right to family life when we are negotiating over services but we need more accessible information on what it really means.

Another difficulty is the assumption that a reference to the Human Rights Act anticipates legal proceedings. But it should be possible to make a claim of rights outside the context of litigation. Perhaps it depends on how the claim is phrased. Reference to statutes can imply that legal action is inevitable whereas reference to principles may not. For example, a tenants association might complain to a landlord about harassment. It may not be necessary to cite the Protection from Eviction Act. In the same way, it may be sufficient to refer to the right to private or family life rather than characterising the situation as a breach of the Human Rights Act. It is one thing to seek to persuade a public authority to comply with the law and another to assert that it has already broken the law. The right approach will depend on the circumstances but the latter statement is likely to lead to the involvement of lawyers.

Encouraging public authorities to adopt a positive approach towards human rights principles should bring results because it complements the messages that the authorities are themselves receiving from the

Government and the inspectorates and in the future, from the Commission for Equality and Human Rights.

Advice and representation

Many voluntary sector advice organisations pursue complaints on behalf of clients and may represent them both through complaint procedures and when they are subject to legal action at tribunals and local courts. This function is shared with law centres and some solicitor firms. The Community Legal Service is also designed to operate in this area. It is clear that people often ask for legal advice, 'not necessarily in order to litigate, but so that they have a firmer basis for their position.' They are lucky if they receive the legal advice that they need. It has been reported that despite the £1.9 billion spent on legal aid in 2002/3, 74 per cent of law firms reported that they turned clients away (due either to limited funds or limited capacity). 'Advice deserts' are common, both in terms of geographical coverage and areas of expertise (Constitutional Affairs Committee, 2004). The reality of cutbacks in legal aid funding is exemplified by one seminar participant's experience:

> Communities want access to legal advice and legal remedies. We had a case recently and we tried 25 different firms of solicitors but not one could take it on. Legal remedies can't be accessed.

Assuming advice and representation services are available, there is potential for using human rights arguments in these procedures. Available evidence on how effectively these are deployed, however, is not encouraging. In a study among 21 solicitors practising law in a socially and economically deprived community in a South Wales valley, published in February 2004, researchers from Cardiff University found that the Human Rights Act 'is not being used to its potential.' The following findings emerged from interviews with solicitors involved in the research:

- 'The Human Rights Act seemed to be accorded symbolic value...rather than being used as a line of reasoning of substance.'

- 'It was seen by some to be a 'last resort tactic' to shore up a weak case.'

- '[The Act] is used less now than when it first came into force.'

- '[Solicitors felt] they were perceived to be attempting to complicate the case, or to delay it.'

- 'Some considered that the courts pay 'lip service' to the Act, making mechanistic reference to it in order to avert a potential ground of appeal.'

- '[The Act is perceived to be more] for the benefit of defendants, at the expense of victims.'

- '[It is perceived to be] relevant only to 'high profile'...issues such as euthanasia, the use of torture and responses to terrorism.'

- 'The training that solicitors had received was insufficiently practical.'

- 'During training, solicitors had been warned about using the Human Rights Act in a frivolous manner.'

- 'Difficulties in legal aid availability [were] a disincentive for clients to pursue human rights issues' (Costigan, 2004).

The study in South Wales described itself as being 'premised on the belief that social justice can be promoted through law and, in particular, through the Human Rights Act.' It is evident that considerable work needs to be done to educate both the legal profession and the judiciary about the role that the Act can play in strengthening rather than undermining social justice cases.

9 Conclusions and recommendations

The Human Rights Act has the potential to contribute to achieving social justice. This proposition is neither widely understood nor accepted. To date, the focus on human rights has been more on atrocities abroad, civil liberties at home, celebrities and court cases than on cultural change within our public service institutions. The opportunity to harness human rights for social justice purposes outside a litigation context has scarcely been recognised, not least by many organisations in the voluntary sector. Yet, ironically, it is the voluntary sector that occupies an optimum position across the spectrum from individuals using public services to public authorities providing them, to introduce human rights principles with the aim of improving the way in which those services are provided. Without active engagement from the voluntary sector, it is likely that socially excluded and vulnerable people will continue to be unable to achieve protection of their human rights. The question for the voluntary sector is how to make this engagement effectively. What can they do and how can they find out about it?

Human rights are a complex and slippery concept for most people to grasp. There has been an absence of political leadership and guidance to make possible a common understanding and acceptance of human rights. The Government has now committed itself to establishing a commission for equality and human rights and the new body will undoubtedly have this function, among other competing functions. But action needs to be taken in the meantime and this should prepare the ground for the commission's work when it is established.

Our findings were that most voluntary sector organisations working on disadvantage and social exclusion described themselves as 'rights-based' and saw that human rights principles are relevant to their work. Many, however, were struggling to use the Human Rights Act to good effect. The Act is potentially a tool but often seems too woolly to use. We found a wide range of responses within sectors and between sectors and between large and small organisations. For example, children's groups and disability groups are often confident in expressly articulating human rights concepts whereas in social care or housing it is less evident. Our objective has been to encourage a connection between the concept of 'human rights' with, for example, the concepts of 'equal rights' and 'empowerment', which are already fundamental to voluntary sector strategies. Although much of the evidence referred to here describes the difficulties that have been encountered, the overall finding was that most voluntary organisations wanted to use a human rights approach and were keen to explore the way in which it could be effectively employed.

We recognise that 'human rights' when applied to our own society remain, at present, confusing for many people. In some quarters, particularly among sections of the media, human rights are distinctly unpalatable. The unfamiliarity with and unpopularity of human rights call for different and often subtle approaches, depending on the circumstances, but they can still be 'rights-based.' No one will disagree with the requirement to accord people dignity and respect but our contention is that this principle is founded on people's human rights rather than just their needs. Dignity and respect represent values to be adhered to and are sufficiently concrete principles to guide the way in which public services are provided. They may lack specificity when relied on in discussions with policy-makers but they should underpin those discussions. Human rights principles should be capable of being confidently referred to without the need to consult lawyers. They should provide the language, which may or may not win an argument, but will at least ensure that the debate is had within a human rights framework.

But the voluntary sector, in general, remains poorly informed about human rights and their connection with existing work on behalf of vulnerable and excluded people. There is considerable work to be done to communicate a vision of human rights that make them more meaningful and useful so that they can be used on behalf of the disadvantaged and vulnerable groups whom the Human Rights Act was supposed to protect.

We make the following recommendations:

- There is an urgent need within the voluntary and community sector for accessible and practical information on the Human Rights Act and underlying human rights principles and how to use them in practice. The impetus for this work should come from the Government as much as from the sector itself and will require vision, leadership and resources.

- Ways in which to disseminate information on human rights within the voluntary sector could include:

  - proactive engagement by voluntary sector membership organisations to disseminate information to their members;

  - web based and other information provision on both cases decided in the courts but also changes that have been achieved in practice without litigation;

  - developing coalitions and alliances which are committed to using equalities and human rights principles and which can focus on the particular needs of the relevant sector.

- Voluntary and community organisations should explore whether designing and adopting a human rights framework could present opportunities to advance the interests of their client groups. This framework would incorporate principles of autonomy, participation and empowerment as well as those from the Human Rights Act. (See chapter 4.)

- Voluntary and community sector organisations should consider using human rights language and emphasising positive obligations when working with public authorities, whether policy-makers or professionals providing services, to seek change and promote accountability for human rights outside a litigation environment.

- Using human rights more explicitly in advocacy and development work with service providers is particularly recommended because:

  - negotiating with service providers is within the capacity of most voluntary organisations;

  - after initial training, using human rights should not be too resource intensive because it is more about an approach to a problem rather than expert knowledge of human rights law;

  - it should be possible to hold public authorities to account for their responsibilities without going to court;

  - there is an opportunity now because this approach complements the message that public authorities are getting, currently from the Audit Commission and others and in the future from the CEHR;

  - it has the potential to achieve the widest reach because of the numbers of people likely to be affected and therefore it can engender cultural change.

  Methods of working include:

  - collaboration with the public sector using existing mechanisms like local strategic partnerships, community cohesion programmes; and

  - development of best practice codes.

- Government has a responsibility to provide leadership and consistency by:

  - adopting proactive measures to provide information and support to the voluntary and community organisations so that they can understand and use human rights principles in their work;

  - promoting public debate about the meaning, purpose and value of human rights principles in society and the role of the Human Rights Act as a tool that can contribute to achieving social justice;

- emphasising that the accountability of public authorities for their human rights responsibilities should not have to be achieved through legal proceedings;

- joining up thinking within Whitehall so that experiences of positive approaches to compliance with human rights and promotion of a culture of respect for human rights are shared between government departments; and

- maintaining and publicising a consistent human rights and equalities message across all government departments.

The Commission for Equality and Human Rights will have a significant role to play in contributing to the work that needs to be done. Being neither a government agency nor a voluntary organisation, it will occupy an independent space and have to use its judgement on where it can make the most difference. It will have a symbiotic relationship with the voluntary and community sector because it will rely on information provided but will also undertake a support function. It should be creative in bringing the voluntary and statutory sectors together to enhance greater understanding of human rights and better compliance with legal responsibilities.

The Human Rights Act presents an opportunity for the voluntary sector to rethink its approach to tackling discrimination and disadvantage. There is firmer ground for using approaches based on rights rather than needs now that there is domestic legislation that can support them. Human rights need not be thought of in narrow and restrictive terms. Aside from litigation, human rights should be a helpful tool for users and their representatives in negotiating with public authorities for better conditions and treatment in individual cases as well as in wider policy campaigns. The purpose of the Human Rights Act is to be a civilising measure, which should enhance the credibility of an argument rather than to diminish it. Human rights principles should inform the way in which policies are made and services provided and the voluntary and community sector can play an important part in ensuring that this is done. The consequences should be greater respect for vulnerable and marginalised people. These are the people who need human rights protection and for whom the Human Rights Act was surely passed.

Appendix 1 A short guide to the Convention rights relevant to this publication which are protected by the Human Rights Act

This is an elementary and selective introduction to the meaning of certain ECHR rights contained in the Human Rights Act (known as 'Convention rights'). The information should be regarded as a starting point for further inquiry. It emphasises the social justice/public services aspects of human rights which are within the scope of the report and so likely to be relevant to readers. It therefore excludes criminal justice (Article 7 and most of Articles 5 and 6) and employment rights (Article 4). Nor does it focus on legal remedies, compensation or procedure.

Both Strasbourg court and UK court decisions are referred to where they have interpreted Convention rights. Not all the cases mentioned resulted in a win by the applicant but they are mentioned because of the principles involved. Where case references are not provided, they will be listed in the References.

Voluntary organisations need to assess which aspects of their work may be affected by Convention rights and then seek further information (some recommended sources are listed in Appendix 2).

Convention rights

Principles to bear in mind in addition to those mentioned in Chapter 1 of the report:

- 'The very essence of the Convention is respect for human dignity and human freedom', quoted in (*Pretty v UK*, ECHR 2346/02).

- The Convention is regarded as a 'living instrument' which means that it moves with the times and reflects progressive social attitudes (e.g. rights of same sex couples and transsexuals).

- Convention rights are to be looked at together as they complement each other.

- Rights fall into different categories.

  - Absolute rights: life (Article 2) and freedom from degrading treatment (Article 3).

  - Unqualified rights: liberty (Article 5), fair trial (Article 6), freedom of thought, conscience and religion (Article 9 (1); but not manifestation which is qualified); marry and found a family (Article 12); access to education (Protocol 1, Article 2).

- Qualified rights: respect for private & family life (Article 8), manifestation of religion (Article 9(2)), expression (Article 10), assembly & association (Article 11) and property (Protocol 1, Article 1).

- Freedom from discrimination (Article 14) is only available in association with another Convention right.

Absolute rights

Absolute rights may not be restricted or balanced with any general public interest. As a consequence, the courts define them narrowly.

Article 2: right to life

'Everyone's right to life shall be protected by law.'

To enforce this right, public authorities may need to take appropriate steps to protect and safeguard the lives of people for whom they are responsible and conduct proper investigations into their deaths. Circumstances in which the right to life is raised include:

- deaths in custody, e.g. mental health institutions;

- deaths in hospital through negligence;

- withdrawing life-saving support/passive euthanasia; see under Articles 3 & 8;

- protection of victims of crime (*Osman v UK* (2000) 29 EHRR 245).

But it should be noted that Article 2 does not extend to a right to die through active euthanasia (Diane Pretty's case) or to a right to life saving treatment whatever the cost (but see under Article 14 below).

Article 3: freedom from degrading and inhuman treatment

'No one shall be subjected to torture or to inhuman or degrading treatment of punishment.'

The key element to Article 3 is dignity. Courts will consider the following factors in deciding whether this right has been breached:

- duration of the treatment, its physical and/or mental effects and, in some cases, the sex, age and state of health of the victim;

- whether the object is to humiliate or debase the person concerned;

- whether the treatment has adversely affected the individual or his/her personality (such as to arouse feelings of fear, anguish and inferiority) (*Keenan v UK* (2001) 33 EHRR 38);

- treatment can be degrading even though person is unconscious of it (R (*Burke*) *v General Medical Council* (2004) EWHC 1879 (Admin)).

Examples of Article 3 application:

- corporal punishment (9 year old boy beaten with garden cane by step-father, *A v UK* (1999) 27 EHRR 611);

- blanket ban on manual handling of disabled people; dignity is a 'core value of society' (*East Sussex* case);

- treatment of vulnerable people in institutions (e.g. older people, children and young people and disabled people in residential or care homes);

- standard of domiciliary care provision;

- compulsory administration or withdrawal of healthcare treatment/right to die with dignity (*Burke* case, above).

Unqualified rights

These rights are unqualified however some are expressly limited.

Article 5: right to liberty
'Everyone has the right to liberty and security of the person.'

The relevant specified limitation here is designed for the individual's own protection:

- 'lawful detention of persons for the prevention of the spreading of infectious diseases, or persons of unsound mind, alcoholics or drug addicts or vagrants' (Article 5(1)(e));

- it is for the authorities to prove that someone is 'of unsound mind' to justify detention (*Mental Health RT* case);

- legal arrangements must be in place to justify detention even where a person has consented to being detained (*Bournewood* case).

Article 6: right to a fair hearing
This right is narrow; it applies to the 'determination of civil rights and obligations' and requires 'fair and public hearing within a reasonable time by an impartial and independent tribunal established by law.'

It is limited to particular situations rather than general application, for example:

- planning procedures;

- confiscation of property or restriction on enjoyment of property;

- decisions to place a child in care and parental access to children in care;

- adoption and fostering;

- medical negligence;

- claims for welfare benefits where the entitlement is established (in contrast to claims where the payment of benefits is discretionary, because of the need to be determining a 'civil right').

Article 9(1): right to freedom of thought, conscience and religion

This right includes conduct that directly expresses a religion or belief, such as the right to a particular diet. But see below regarding manifestation of this right.

Article 12: right to marry and found a family

Marriage has been interpreted as a legally binding association between a man and a woman. The right under this article:

- has not protected the rights of gay and lesbian couples;

- has protected the right of transsexuals to marry (*Goodwin v UK* (2002) EHRR 447).

Protocol 1, Article 2: right of access to education

'No one shall be denied the right to education.'

There are special provisions about education according to parent or child's religious and philosophical beliefs (e.g. jilbab, *Begum* case). This right has been invoked in cases of children with special needs (*Simpson v UK* (1989) 64 DR 188).

Qualified rights

These rights may be qualified provided the restriction satisfies each of the following conditions:

- has a clear legal basis;

- has a legitimate aim (listed below under each Article);

- is necessary in a democratic society which means: fulfils a pressing social need, and; is 'proportionate' (i.e. the restriction should only go as far as is needed to achieve the objective and must not be overly restrictive) and;

- must not discriminate (see Article 14 below).

Applying a qualified right requires balancing the interests of the individuals/groups claiming it with those of other individuals/groups or the needs of society as a whole.

Article 8: right to respect for private and family life, home and correspondence
Includes:

General principles:

- bodily integrity and dignity (*East Sussex* case);
- personal autonomy (with regard to treatment when person is near death) (*Burke* case, above);
- Article 8 'extends to features which are integral to a person's identity or ability to function socially as a person' (*R (Razgar) v SSHD* [2004] 3 WLR 58).

Specific application:

- rights of residents when care homes are closed (*Madden* case);
- disabled woman's right to housing (*Bernard* case);
- housing for travellers and gypsies (*Connors v UK* ECHR 66746/01);
- freedom to express one's sexuality;
- identity issues relating to gender reassignment;
- consent to medical treatment;
- personal information held by public authorities (*Gaskin v UK* (1989) 12 EHRR 36);
- CCTV and video recordings;
- immigration;
- adoption and custody of children;
- exposure to environmental pollution (waste treatment plant (*Lopez Ostra v Spain* (1994) 20 EHHR 277, radiation from nuclear plant (*McGinley v UK* (1998) 27 EHRR 1).

But has not included:

- right to financial assistance to enable parents to stay at home and care for their children (*AP v Austria* (1995) 20 EHRR CD 63);
- right to caravan place for Romany gypsy woman suffering from cancer (*Burton v UK* (1996) 22 EHRR CD 134).

Grounds for restriction:

- national security;

- public safety;

- economic well-being of the country (e.g. immigration controls; argument against banning night flights *Hatton v UK* (2003) 37 EHRR 611);

- prevention of crime;

- protection of health and morals;

- protection of the rights and freedoms of others (e.g. rights of children not to be abused by their parents (Article 3) balanced against parents' rights to family life (Article 8) (*Bedfordshire CC* case);

Article 9 (2): freedom to manifest religion or belief
Grounds for restriction:

- public safety;

- protection of public order, health or morals;

- protection of rights and freedoms of others.

Article 10: freedom of expression
Grounds for restriction:

- national security;

- public safety;

- prevention of disorder or crime – e.g. incitement to racial hatred;

- protection of health and morals – e.g. censorship;

- protection of the rights and reputations of others – e.g. libel laws;

- preventing the disclosure of information received in confidence – e.g. data protection.

Article 11: freedom of assembly and association
Grounds for restriction:

- national security;

- public safety;

- prevention of disorder or crime – e.g. public order laws;

- protection of health and morals;

- protection of the rights and reputations of others.

Protocol 1, Article 1: right to peaceful enjoyment of possessions
This right includes some welfare benefits but caution is needed because it is a complicated area.

Restrictions:

- public interest;

- subject to conditions provided for by law: permanent (taxation and compulsory purchase of property) and, temporary (removing car, taking away driving licence).

Associated or 'conjunctive right

Article 14: freedom from discrimination in enjoyment of convention rights
Specified grounds: sex, race, colour, language, religion, political or other opinion, national or social origin, association with a national minority, property, birth or other status;

- must relate to other Convention right (e.g. arguments about 'postcode lottery' of NHS funding if certain life-saving treatments not available in predominantly BME areas but are available in other geographical areas, could argue violation of Article 2 and 14);

- 'other status' is interpreted as including sexual orientation (*Ghaidan* case);

- positive discrimination may be allowed if reasonably and objectively justified.

Appendix 2 **Recommended information sources**

The information given here supplements and does not repeat the written materials referred to in the list of references.

Further publications

Crossman G and Wadham J (eds) (2000) *Your Rights* Liberty, www.yourrights.org.uk [new edition (8th) due January 2005, Morrow P and Addis M (eds)]

Daw R (2000) *The Impact of the Human Rights Act for Disabled People*, Disability Rights Commission, www.drc-gb.org/thelaw/humanrights.asp

Drew S (2000) *Children and the Human Rights Act*, Save the Children, www.savethechildren.org.uk

Help the Aged (2000) *The Human Rights Act: What are the implications for older people?*, www.helptheaged.org.uk

Starmer K (1999) *European Human Rights Law*, Legal Action Group, www.lag.org.uk

Watson J and Woolf M (2003) *Human Rights Act Toolkit*, Legal Action Group, www.lag.org.uk

Human rights organisations

British Institute of Human Rights
The Law School, King's College London,
26–29 Drury Lane, London WC2B 5RL
Tel: 020 7848 1818
Fax: 020 7848 1814
Email: admin@bihr.org
Website: http://www.bihr.org

Committee for the Administration of Justice
45/47 Donegall Street, Belfast BT1 2BR,
Northern Ireland
Tel: 028-90961122
Fax: 028-90246706
Email: info@caj.org.uk
Website: http://www.caj.org.uk

Liberty
21 Tabard Street, London SE1 4LA
Tel: 020 7403 3888
Fax: 020 7407 5354
Email: info@liberty-human-rights.org.uk
Website: http://www.liberty-human-rights.org.uk

Justice
59 Carter Lane, London EC4V 5AQ
Tel: 020 7329 5100
Fax: 020 7329 5055
Email: admin@justice.org.uk
Website: http://www.justice.org.uk

1990 Trust
Room 12, Winchester House, 9 Cranmer Road,
Kennington Park, London SW9 6EJ
Tel: 020 7582 1990
Fax: 020 7793 8269
Email: blink1990@blink.org.uk
Website: http://www.blink.org.uk

Scottish Human Rights Centre
146 Holland Street,Glasgow G2 4NG
Tel: 0141 332 59 60
Fax: 0141 332 53 09
Email: shrc@dial.pipex.com

Membership organisations and coalitions
Children's Rights Alliance for England
94 White Lion Street, London N1 9PF
Tel: 020 7278 8222
Fax: 020 7278 9552
Email: info@crae.org.uk
Website: http://www.crae.org.uk

Consortium of Lesbian, Gay and Bisexual Voluntary and Community
Organisations
2 Plough Yard, Shoreditch High Street, London EC2A 3LP
Tel: 020 7422 8611
Fax: 020 7426 0051
Email: info@clgb.org.uk
Website: http://www.lgbconsortium.org.uk

End Child Poverty Campaign
8 Wakley Street, London EC1V 7QE
Tel: 020 7843 1913
Fax: 020 7843 1918
Email: info@ecpc.org.uk
Website: http://www.ecpc.org.uk

Equal and Diverse North East
c/o One North East, Stella House,Goldcrest Way, Newburn Riverside,
Newcastle-upon-Tyne NE15 8NY
Fax: 01665 576163
Email: julia@positivedifference.org
Website: http://www.positivedifference.org

Equality and Diversity Forum
207-221 Pentonville Road, London N1 9UZ
Tel: 020 7843 1597
Fax: 020 7843 1599
Email: Equalityforum@taen.org.uk
Website: http://www.equalitydiversityforum.org.uk

Equality Coalition
c/o Fawcett Society, 1-3 Berry Street,
London EC1V 0AA
Tel: 020 7253 2598
Fax: 020 7253 2599
Email: info@equalities.org
Website: http://www.equalities.org

NCVO
National Council for Voluntary Organisations,
Regent's Wharf, 8 All Saints Street, London N1 9RL
Switchboard: 020 7713 6161
HelpDesk: 0800 2798 798
Email: HelpDesk@ncvo-vol.org.uk
Website: www.ncvo-vol.org.uk

Scottish Voluntary Sector Equality and Human Rights Coalition
Equality Team SCVO, 3rd floor, Centrum Building,
38 Queen Street, Glasgow G1 3DX
Tel: 0141 221 0030
Fax: 0141 248 8066
Email: denise.gildea@scvo.org.uk
Website: http://www.scvo.org.uk/equalities/contact_us/index.htm

The Traveller Law Reform Coalition
Banderway House, 156-162 Kilburn High Road,
London, NW6 4JD
Tel: 020 7625 2255
Email: romanistan@yahoo.com
Website: http://www.travellerslaw.org.uk

Welsh Equalities and Human Rights Coalition
c/o The Welsh Council for Voluntary Action
Tel: 0870 607 1666
Email: help@wcva.org.uk
Website: http://www.cggc.org.uk

Equality and human rights commissions
Commission for Racial Equality (CRE)
St Dunstan's House, 201-211 Borough High Street,
London SE1 1GZ
Tel: 020 7939 0000
Fax: 020 7939 0001
Email: info@cre.gov.uk
Website: http://www.cre.gov.uk

Disability Rights Commission (DRC)
DRC Helpline, FREEPOST MID02164, Stratford upon Avon CV37 9BR
Tel: 08457 622 633
Textphone: 08457 622 644
Website: http://www.drc-gb.org

Equal Opportunities Commission (EOC)
Arndale House, Arndale Centre, Manchester M4 3EQ
Fax: 0161 838 1733
Tel: 0845 601 5901
Email: info@eoc.org.uk
Website: http://www.eoc.org.uk

Equality Commission for Northern Ireland
Equality House, 7-9 Shaftesbury Square, Belfast BT2 7DP
Tel: 028 90 500600
Fax: 028 90 248687
Textphone: 028 90 500589
Email: information@equalityni.org
Website: http://www.equalityni.org

Northern Ireland Human Rights Commission
Temple Court, 39 North Street, Belfast BT1 1NA
Tel: 028 9024 3987
Fax: 028 9024 7844
Email: info@nihrc.org
Website: http://www.nihrc.org

Government Departments

Department for Constitutional Affairs, Human Rights Division
Selborne House, 54 Victoria Street, London SW1E 6QW
Tel: 020 7210 1437
Email: humanrights@dca.gsi.gov.uk.

Department for Trade and Industry, Women and Equality Unit
35 Great Smith Street, London SW1P 3BQ
Tel: 0845 001 0029
Email: info-womenandequalityunit@dti.gsi.gov.uk
Website: http://www.womenandequalityunit.gov.uk

Home Office, Active Communities Directorate
3rd Floor, Allington Towers, 19 Allington Street, London SW1E 5EB
Tel: 020 7035 5328
Fax: 020 7035 5386
Email: public_enquiries.acu@homeoffice.gsi.gov.uk
Website: http://www.homeoffice.gov.uk/comrace/index.html

Inspectorates

Audit Commission
1st Floor, Millbank Tower, Millbank, London SW1P 4HQ
Tel: 020 7828 1212
Textphone: 020 7630 0421
Fax: 020 7976 6187
Website: http://www.audit-commission.gov.uk

Healthcare Commission
Finsbury Tower, 103-105 Bunhill Row, London EC1Y 8TG
Tel: 020 7448 9200
Email: feedback@healthcarecommission.org.uk
Website: http://www.healthcarecommission.org.uk

Parliament

Joint Committee on Human Rights
Committee Office, House of Commons, 7 Millbank, London SW1P 3JA
Tel: 020 7219 2797
Fax: 020 7219 8393
Email: jchr@parliament.uk
Website: http://www.parliament.uk/parliamentary_committees/
joint_committee_on_human_rights.cfm

References

Audit Commission (2003) *Human rights: improving public service delivery*, www.audit-commission.gov.uk/reports

Beirne M (2004) 'Socio-Economic Rights as Agents for Change' in Harvey C (ed) *Human Rights in the Community* BIHR/Hart, forthcoming

Brownlie I (ed) (1994) *Basic Documents on Human Rights* Clarendon

Bynoe I (1997) *Rights to Fair Treatment: A Practical Study to Develop New Rights for People Seeking Health or Social Care* IPPR

CESCR (2001) *Statement on Poverty and the ICESCR E/C.12/2001/10*, www.unhchr.ch/tbs/doc.nsf/(Symbol)/E.C.12.2001.10.En

Charity Commission (2003) *The Promotion of Human Rights*, www.charity-commission.gov.uk/publications/ccpubs3.asp

CLS (2004) *The Human Rights Act: what it means for you*, Information leaflet No. 7, www.clsdirect.org.uk

Constitutional Affairs Committee (2004) *Civil Legal Aid: adequacy of provision*, 4th report, session 2003-04 HC 391-I, www.publications.parliament.uk/pa/cm/cmconst.htm

Costigan R, Sheehan J and Thomas PA (2004) *The Human Rights Act 1998: An Impact Study in South Wales*, Cardiff Law School

Dalrymple T (2004) 'Wronged by our rights' *Spectator*, 24 April 2004

DCA (2002) *Study Guide, Human Rights Act 1998*, 2nd edition, www.humanrights.gov.uk/studyguide

DCA (2004) Interdepartmental review of International Human Rights Instruments, www.dca.gov.uk/hract/ngo/review_2002.htm

DFID (2004) *Key sheets for sustainable livelihoods, Policy and Implementation, Section 18: rights-based approaches*, www.keysheets.org

DTI (2004) *Fairness for All: A New Commission for Equality and Human Rights*, White Paper, www.dti.gov.uk/publications

DTI (2004) *£1.3m to spread the word on equality*, press release on Employment Equality (sexual orientation and religion or belief) Regulations, Jacqui Smith MP, deputy minister for women, 11 June 2004, www.gnn.gov.uk

Hale B (2004), *What can the Human Rights Act do for my mental health?* BIHR Sieghart memorial lecture, www.bihr.org

Health Committee (2003) *Elder Abuse*, 2nd report, session 2003-04 HC 111, www.parliament.uk/parliamentary_committees/health_committee

Home Office (1998) *Compact on Relations between Government and the Voluntary and Community Sector in England*, Home Office Voluntary and Community Unit www.homeoffice.gov.uk and Working Group on Government Relations www.ncvo-vol.org.uk

Home Office (2000) *A New Era of Rights and Responsibilities: Core Guidance for Public Authorities*, www.humanrights.gov.uk/coregd.htm

Home Office (2000) *Private Sector Public Service: Human Rights for All*; www.humanrights.gov.uk/ppintro.htm

JCHR (2001) *Minutes of Evidence taken on Monday 19 March 2001: Implementation of the Human Rights Act 1998, The Lord Chancellor, Rt Hon The Lord Irvine of Lairg*, 19.03.01, HL 66-ii HC 332-ii, www.parliament.uk/parliamentary_committees/joint_committee_on_human_rights.cfm

JCHR (2002) *The Case for a Human Rights Commission: Interim Report*, 22nd report, session 2001-02, HL 160 HC 1142, www.parliament.uk/parliamentary_committees/joint_committee_on_human_rights.cfm

JCHR (2003) *The Case for a Human Rights Commission*, 6th report, session 2002-03 HL 67-I HC 489-I, www.parliament.uk/parliamentary_committees/joint_committee_on_human_rights.cfm

JCHR (2003) *The Case for a Children's Commissioner for England*, 9th report, session 2002-03 HL 96 HC 666, www.parliament.uk/parliamentary_committees/joint_committee_on_human_rights.cfm

JCHR (2003) *UN Convention on the Rights of the Child*, 10th report, session 2002-03; HL 117 HC 81, www.parliament.uk/parliamentary_committees/joint_committee_on_human_rights.cfm

JCHR (2003) *Work of the Northern Ireland Human Rights Commission*, 14th report, session 2002-03, HL 132 HC 142, www.parliament.uk/parliamentary_committees/joint_committee_on_human_rights.cfm

JCHR (2004) *The Meaning of Public Authority under the Human Rights Act*, 7th report, session 2003-04, HL 39 HC 382, www.parliament.uk/parliamentary_committees/joint_committee_on_human_rights.cfm

JCHR (2004) *Commission for Equality and Human Rights: Structure, Functions and Powers*, 11th report session 2003-04, HL 78 HC 536, www.parliament.uk/parliamentary_committees/joint_committee_on_human_rights.cfm

JCHR (2004) *The International Covenant on Economic, Social and Cultural Rights*, 21st report, session 2003-04, HL 183/HC 1188, www.parliament.uk/parliamentary_committees/joint_committee_on_human_rights.cfm

Klug F (2000) *Values for a Godless Age. The Story of the United Kingdom's New Bill of Rights* Penguin

Lister R (2004) *Poverty and Social Justice* Bevan Foundation Annual Lecture June 2004

NCVO (2000) *Impact of the Human Rights Act 1998 on Voluntary Organisations, an NCVO briefing* NCVO Publications

NCVO (2004) Wilding K et al. 'The UK Voluntary Sector Alamanac 2004' NCVO Publications

Pleasence, Pascoe, Buck, Balmer, O'Grady, Genn, and Smith (2004) *Causes of Action: Civil Law and Social Justice* HMSO

Royal College of Nursing and The Maternity Alliance (2004) joint briefing on *Health and Social Care (Community Health and Standards) Bill*, House of Lords Report Stage

Ruxton S and Karim R (2001) *Beyond Civil Rights: Developing Economic, Social and Cultural Rights in the United Kingdom*, Oxfam/JUSTICE, www.oxfam.org.uk/what_we_do/resources/civilrights.html

Shelter (2004) *Toying with their future: the hidden cost of the housing crisis*, www.shelter.org.uk/ policy/policy-825.cfm/plitem/141/

State of the Nation (2000) *Joseph Rowntree Reform Trust/ICM State of the Nation Poll*, www.icmresearch.co.uk/reviews/2000/state-of-the-nation-2000.htm

Straw J (1999) *Building a Human Rights Culture*, speech to Civil Service College seminar 9.12.99, www.dca.gov.uk/hract/cscspe.htm

Victim Support (2003) *The Human Rights Act and its implication for victims and witnesses*, www.victimsupport.org.uk

Watson J (2002) *Something for Everyone: The impact of the Human Rights Act and the need for a Human Rights Commission* BIHR, www.bihr.org

Cases

Bedfordshire CC case, Z v UK (2002) 34 EHRR 3

Begum case, R (Begum) v Headteacher and Governors of Denbigh High School, [2004] EWHC 1389 (Admin), [2004] ELR 374

Bournewood case, H.L. v the United Kingdom (application no. 45508/99), ECtHR, October 2004

East Sussex case, R v East Sussex County Council & DRC, ex parte A, B, X and Y [2003] EHC 167 (Admin)

Leonard Cheshire case, Callin, Heather and Ward v Leonard Cheshire Foundation [2002] EWCA Civ 366

Limbuela case, SSHD v Limbuela, Tesema and Adam [2004] EWCA Civ 540

Madden case, R (Madden) v Bury Metropolitan Borough Council [2002] EWHC 1882 (Admin)

Mental Health RT case, R (H) v Mental Health Review Tribunal [2001] EWCA Civ 415

Partnerships in Care case, R (A) v Partnerships in Care Ltd [2002] 1WLR 2610

R v A case [2001] UKHL 25

Z, A & R cases [2001] Imm AR 560